The Road And The Roadside

by

Burton Willis Potter

Double9 BOOKS

The Road And The Roadside
by Burton Willis Potter

ISBN: 978-93-71812-32-0

Published by

DOUBLE 9 BOOKS
2/13-B, Ansari Road
Daryaganj, New Delhi – 110002
info@double9books.com
www.double9books.com
Tel. 011-40042856

ABOUT THE AUTHOR

Burton Willis Potter is best known for his work The Road and the Roadside, which reflects his deep interest in public infrastructure and its role in the progress of society. Potter's writing combines practical guidance with historical and legal context, emphasizing the social value of well-maintained roads and responsible civic planning. He often highlighted the importance of good governance and public responsibility in managing communal resources. Though specific details about his early life, education, or broader career remain limited, his focus on Massachusetts law and local government indicates he was likely involved in legal or municipal work within that state. His ability to connect historical precedent with contemporary legal practices suggests a thorough academic background. Potter's parents are not widely documented in public records, and much of his legacy rests on his contributions to civic literature. His work remains a reflection of the growing awareness in the late 19th century of infrastructure as a key to democratic stability and economic growth.

CONTENTS

PREFACE

The chapters of this book relating to the laws of public and private ways were written and read as a lecture at the Country Meeting of the Massachusetts Board of Agriculture, in December, 1885, at Framingham, and have since been published in the "Report on the Agriculture of Massachusetts for the Year 1885."

The laws as herein stated are, as I believe, the present laws of Massachusetts relative to public and private ways, and therefore they may not all be applicable to the ways in other States; but inasmuch as the common law is the basis of the road law in all the States, it will be found that the general principles herein laid down are as applicable in one State as in another.

Believing that good roads and the love of rural life are essential to the true happiness and lasting prosperity of any people, these pages have been written with the sincere desire to do something to improve our roads and to encourage country life; and they are now given to the public with the hope that they will exert some little influence in promoting these objects.

B. W. P.

Worcester, Mass.,
May, 1886.

CHAPTER I
HISTORY, IMPORTANCE, AND SIGNIFICANCE OF ROADS

The development of the means of communication between different communities, peoples, and races has ever been coexistent with the progress of civilization. Lord Macaulay declares that of all inventions, the alphabet and printing-press alone excepted, those inventions which abridge distance have done most for the civilization of our species. Every improvement of the means of locomotion benefits mankind morally and intellectually as well as materially.

"The road," Bushnell says, "is that physical sign or symbol by which you will best understand any age or people. If they have no roads, they are savages; for the road is the creation of man and a type of civilized society. If you wish to know whether society is stagnant, learning scholastic, religion a dead formality, you may learn something by going into universities and libraries, something also by the work that is doing on cathedrals and churches or in them, but quite as much by looking at the roads; for if there is any motion in society, the road, which is the symbol of motion, will indicate the fact."

As roads are the symbols of progress, so, according to the philosophy of Carlyle, they should only be used by working and progressive people, as he asserts that the public highways ought not to be occupied by people demonstrating that motion is impossible. Hence, when we trace back the history of the race to the dawn of civilization, we find that the first sponsors of art and science, commerce and manufacture, education and government, were the builders and supporters of public highways.

The two most ancient civilizations situated in the valleys of the Nile and the Euphrates were connected by a commercial and military highway leading from Babylon to Memphis, along which passed the war chariots and the armies of the great chieftains and military kings of ancient days, and over which were carried the gems, the gold, the spices, the ivories, the textile fabrics, and all the curious and unrivalled productions of the luxurious Orient. On the line of this roadway arose Nineveh, Palmyra, Damascus, Tyre, Antioch, and other great commercial cities.

On the southern shores of the Mediterranean the Carthaginians built up and consolidated an empire so prominent in military and naval achievements and in the arts and industries of civilized life, that for four hundred years it was able to hold its own against the preponderance of Greece and Rome; and as might have been expected, they were systematic and scientific road-makers from whom the Romans learned the art of road-building.

The Romans were apt scholars, and possessed a wonderful capacity not only to utilize prior inventions but also to develop them. They were beyond question the most successful and masterful road-builders in the ancient world; and the perfection of their highways was one of the most potent causes of their superiority in progress and civilization. When they conquered a province they not only annexed it politically, by imposing on its people their laws and system of government, but they annexed it socially and commercially, by the construction of good roads from its chief places to one or more of the great roadways which brought them in easy and direct communication with the metropolis of the Roman world. And when their territory reached from the remote east to the farthest west, and a hundred millions of people acknowledged their military and political supremacy, their capital city was in the centre of such a network of highways that it was then a common saying, "All roads lead to Rome." From the forum of Rome a broad and magnificent highway ran out towards every province of the empire. It was terraced up with sand, gravel, and cement, and covered with stones and granite, and followed in a direct line without regard to the configuration of the country, passing over or under mountains and across streams and lakes, on arches of solid masonry. The military roads were under the pretors, and were called pretorian roads; and the public roads for travel and commercial traffic were under the consuls, and were called consular roads. These roads were kept entirely distinct; the pretorian roads were used for the marching of armies and the transportation of military supplies, and the consular roads were used for traffic and general travel. They were frequently laid out alongside of each other from place to place, very much as railroads and highways are now found side by side. The consular roads were generally twelve feet wide in the travelled pathway, with a raised footway on the side; but sometimes the footway was in the middle of the road, with a carriage-way on each side of it. The military roads were generally sixty feet wide, with an elevated centre, twenty feet wide, and slopes upon either side, also twenty feet wide. Stirrups were not then invented, and mounting stones or blocks were necessary accommodations; and hence the lines of the roads were studded with mounting-blocks and also with milestones. Some of these roads could be travelled to the north and eastward two thousand miles; and they were kept in such good repair that a traveller thereon, by using relays of horses, which were kept on the road, could easily make a hundred miles a day. Far as the eye could see stretched those symbols of her all-conquering and all-attaining influence, which made the most distant provinces a part of her dominions, and connected them with her imperial capital by imperial highways.

The Romans not only had great public highways, but they possessed a complete and systematic network of cross-roads, which connected villages, and brought into communication therewith cultivated farms and prosperous homesteads. In Italy alone it is estimated that they had about fourteen thousand miles of good roads. Their laws relating to the construction and maintenance of highways were founded in reason and a just conception of the uses and objects of public ways; and they are the basis of modern highway legislation. By their law the roads were for the public use and convenience, and their emperors, consuls, and other public officials were their conservators. They were built at the public expense, under the supervision of professional engineers and surveyors, and kept in repair by the districts and provinces through which they passed.

But during the dark ages, when arts were lost, when popular learning disappeared or found shelter only in cloisters and convents, when commercial intercourse between nations vanished, and when civilization itself lay fallen and inert, these magnificent Roman roads were unused and left to the destructive agencies of time and the elements of Nature. Rains and floods washed away and inundated their embankments; forests and rank vegetation overgrew and concealed them; winds covered them with dust and heaps of sand; and little by little in the process of ages their hard surfaces and massive foundations were somewhat broken and caused to partially decay. That their remains still exist in every part of the world which ever bore up the Roman legions is conclusive evidence that they were built by master workmen who realized that they were responsible to posterity and to the eternal powers.

"In the elder days of Art
Builders wrought with greatest care
Each minute and unseen part;
For the gods see everywhere."

In China, at one time, labor was so abundant that it was kept employed in constructing great walls and ponderous roads. The road-bed was raised several feet above the level of the ground by an accumulation of great stones, and then covered with huge granite blocks. It was found that in time the wheels of vehicles wore deep ruts in the stones, while the travelled part of the road became so smooth that it was almost impossible for animals to stand thereon.

In the ancient empires of Mexico and Peru, where there were no beasts fit for draught or for riding, magnificent roads were constructed for the treble purpose of facilitating the march of armies, accommodating the public traffic, and ministering to the convenience and luxury of the lordly rulers. In Peru two of these roads were from fifteen hundred to two thousand miles long, extending from Quito to Chili,—one by the borders of the ocean, and the other over the grand plateau by the mountains. Prescott says: "The road over the plateau was conducted over pathless sierras buried in snow; galleries were cut for leagues through the living rock; rivers were crossed by means of bridges that swung suspended in the air; precipices were scaled by stairways hewn out of the native bed; ravines of hideous depth were filled up with solid masonry; in short, all the difficulties that beset a wild and mountainous region, and which might appall the most courageous engineer of modern times, were encountered and successfully overcome. Stone pillars in the manner of European milestones were erected at stated intervals of somewhat more than a league all along the route. Its breadth scarcely exceeded twenty feet. It was built of heavy flags of freestone, and in some parts, at least, covered with a bituminous cement, which time has made harder than the stone itself. In some places where the ravines had been filled up with masonry, the mountain torrents, wearing on it for ages, have gradually eaten a way through the base, and left the superincumbent mass—such is the cohesion of the materials—still spanning the valley like an arch.

"Another great road of the Incas lay through the level country between the Andes and the ocean. It was constructed in a different manner, as demanded by the nature of the ground, which was for the most part low, and much of it sandy. The causeway was raised on a high embankment of earth, and defended on either side by a parapet or wall of clay; and trees and odoriferous shrubs were planted along the margin, regaling the sense of the traveller with their perfume, and refreshing him by their shades, so grateful under the burning sky of the tropics.

"The care of the great roads was committed to the districts through which they passed, and a large number of hands was constantly employed to keep them in repair. This was the more easily done in a country where the mode of travelling was altogether on foot; though the roads are said to have been so nicely constructed that a carriage might have rolled over them as securely as on any of the great roads of Europe. Still, in a region where the elements of fire and water are both actively at work in the business of destruction, they must without constant supervision have gradually gone to decay. Such has been their fate under the Spanish conquerors, who took no care to enforce the admirable system for their preservation adopted by the Incas. Yet the broken portions that still survive here and there, like the fragments of the great Roman roads scattered over Europe, bear evidence of their primitive grandeur, and have drawn forth eulogium from the discriminating traveller; for Humboldt, usually not profuse in his panegyrics, says, 'The roads of the Incas were among the most useful and stupendous works ever executed by man.'"

With the revival of human thought and civilization after the Middle Ages, the improvement of the roads engaged the attention of public and scientific men, and became once more an object of government; but for a long time the rulers who concerned themselves about roads thought more about repressing the crimes of violence and extortion thereon than they did about improving their condition for travel. The first act of the English Parliament relative to the improvement of roads in the kingdom was in 1523; yet in 1685 most of the roads in England were in a deplorable condition.

Macaulay says that on the best highways at that time the ruts were deep, the descents precipitous, and the way often such that it was hardly possible to distinguish it in the dark from the unenclosed heath and fen which lay on both sides. It was only in fine weather that the whole breadth of the road was available for wheeled vehicles; often the mud lay deep on the right and on the left, and only a narrow track of firm ground rose above the quagmire. It happened almost every day that coaches stuck fast until a team of cattle could be procured from some neighboring farm to tug them out of the slough. But to the honor of England, this condition of her roads was not allowed to continue very long. Although her progress in trade and prosperity has been marvellously rapid, yet such progress can be measured by the improvement of her roads, which are now unsurpassed anywhere in the world.

Beyond question, internal communications are of vital importance to every nation, and good roads are a prime necessity to every town or city. A good road is always a source of comfort and pleasure to every traveller. It is also a source of great saving each year in the wear and tear of horse-flesh, vehicles, and harnesses. Good roads to market and neighbors increase the price of farm produce, and bring people into business relations and good fellowship, and thereby enhance in value every homestead situated in their neighborhood. They cause a proper distribution of population between town and country. For many years in this country there has been a movement of population from the rural districts into the cities and manufacturing villages. Many ancestral homesteads have been deserted for promising "fresh woods and pastures new" in the commercial world. This centralization of population is evidently a violation of economic laws, and when carried too far results in business depression, in the multiplication of tramps, and in the origination and development of industrial and social troubles. The remedy for this state of affairs is found in the readjustment and proper distribution of population between town and country. When men, sick of waiting on waning business prospects, turn to the soil as their only refuge from non-employment and surplus productions of factories, and reoccupy and rehabilitate deserted or run-down farms, then business revives, and the wheels of industry and enterprise revolve steadily and with increased velocity at each revolution. Bad roads have a tendency to make the country disagreeable as a dwelling-place, and a town which is noted for its bad roads is shunned by people in search of rural homes. On the other hand, good roads have a tendency to make the country a desirable dwelling-place, and a town which is noted for its good roads becomes the abode of people of taste, wealth, and intelligence. Hence it behooves every town to make itself a desirable place of residence; for many people are always puzzling themselves over the problem of where and how to live, and those towns which have their floors swept and garnished and their lamps trimmed and burning ready to receive the bride and bridegroom, will be most likely to attract within their borders the seekers of farm life and rural homes. We now live in the city and go to the country; but we should live in the country and go to the city. This is "a consummation devoutly to be wished;" but it can never be brought about until good roads connect the cities and villages with the green fields and beautiful scenery of the country. All money and labor expended upon them result immediately in a convenience and benefit to the whole community. Every one should deem it an honor to be able to do anything to improve and beautify the highways of his town. The Lacedemonian kings were *ex officio* highway surveyors, and among the Thebans the most illustrious citizens were proud to hold that office; and a few years ago Horatio Seymour, of New York, said that his only remaining ambition for public life was to be regarded as the best path-master in Oneida County.

CHAPTER II
LOCATION

When a new road is laid out it is important that it should be located in the best attainable place, considering the natural formation of the surrounding country; for when a highway is once established it is impossible to say how long the tide of humanity and commercial traffic will seek passage over it. While the ordinary processes of Nature—rain, thaw, and frost—are ever at work lowering the hills and mountains and filling up the valleys and lowlands, the public highways of a country remain in the same relative positions from age to age.

The great commercial and military highway which in the early dawn of Roman history led from the banks of the placid Euphrates to the banks of the many-mouthed Nile—over which Abraham once wended his weary steps on his way to Canaan, over which the hosts of Xerxes and the brave phalanxes of Alexander the Great once passed in all the pride and glory of war, over which the wise men of the East probably journeyed in search of him who was born King of the Jews, over which Mary fled with Christ in her flight into Egypt, and along which the early Christians travelled as they went forth to preach the fatherhood of God and the brotherhood of men—is to-day the highway over which is carried on the overland intercourse between the Mediterranean and the Persian Gulf.

Many of the present roads in Italy and the neighboring countries are identical with the roads over which Cæsar, Cicero, and other Romans travelled in the olden days; and the modern British roads are the same, in many cases, as those used by the ancient Britons before the Anglo-Saxon conquest.

The law of the survival of the fittest is applicable to the location of roads, and any well-located road is liable to be used as a public way during the occupancy of the earth by the human race; and if it is not made famous by the passage of illustrious persons or sanctified by the footsteps of saints, yet it is liable to be travelled through coming ages by "mute inglorious Miltons" and by "care-encumbered men." It sometimes happens that men and women, in doing faithfully and well the nearest duty, perform work which turns out better than they expect.

> "The hand that rounded Peter's dome,
> And groined the aisles of Christian Rome,
> Wrought in a sad sincerity;
> He builded better than he knew."

The originators of many great reforms in law and religion, in working to establish principles applicable and needful to local issues, have thereby, unconsciously to themselves, established principles which have proved beneficial and applicable to the whole human race. In the stress of trying times we have discovered in the constitution of our country latent powers which its framers never dreamed were there. Thus it is with the humble occupation of road-building. A road constructed for the convenience of some primitive community or to gratify the caprice of some rich man or lordly ruler becomes often in after years an Appian Way for public travel and commercial intercourse.

A road may be located in one of three ways. It may be laid out in a straight line by crossing lowlands in the mud and going over hills at steep grades. The ancient Britons, like the early settlers in this country, established their homesteads and villages on commanding situations, and ran their roads and bridle-paths in direct courses by their habitations. The Romans, possessors of great wealth and abundant slave-labor, built their military and public roads in direct lines from place to place, regardless of expense. In this way they shortened distances somewhat, but their roads must have been constructed at enormous expense in money and labor. Their roads were marvels of engineering skill and workmanship, which even now, after the lapse of eighteen centuries, impress every thoughtful observer with the idea that he is in the presence of the work of the immortals. They threw arched bridges of solid masonry over rivers and across ravines; they cut tunnels through mountains, and sometimes carried their roads underground for the sole purpose of shelter from the sun; they levelled heights and made deep cuts through hills; and when they came to a marsh they built a causeway high enough and strong enough to make it safe and dry at all seasons of the year. This mode of location is still followed in the Latin countries of Italy, France, and Spain, where many of the roads are identical with the old Roman roads.

The other mode of locating a highway is to seek the best attainable grade the country will permit of by winding through valleys and around and across hills. There is obviously one advantage to a perfectly straight road between two places: *it is the nearest route*. But this is about the only advantage a straight road has over a curved one. In a hilly country a straight road is frequently no shorter than a curved one, because the distance around a hill is generally no greater than over it, as the length of a pail-handle is the same whether it is vertical or in a horizontal position. In an uneven country a straight road with anything like the same grade as the curved road can only be constructed at enormous and unnecessary expense and labor. Even in a level country a road curved sufficiently to give variety of view and to conform to Hogarth's "line of beauty" is preferable to a perfectly straight road, which is always tedious to the traveller.

"The road the human being travels,
That on which blessing comes and goes, doth follow
The river's course, the valley's playful windings,
Curves round the corn-field and the hill of vines."

Moreover, we are told by competent engineers that the difference in length between a straight and a slightly curved road is very small. Thus, if a road between two places ten miles apart was made to curve so that the eye could nowhere see farther than a quarter of a mile of it at once, its length would exceed that of a perfectly straight road between the same points by only about one hundred and fifty yards.

But, in any event, in road-making mere straightness should always yield to a level grade, even if thereby the distance is greatly increased; for on a good grade a horse can draw rapidly and easily a load which it would be impossible for him to draw on a steep grade. It is an accepted maxim by road-engineers that the horizontal length of a road may be advantageously increased, to avoid an ascent, by at least twenty times the perpendicular height which is to be thus saved; that is, to escape a hill a hundred feet high, it would be proper for the road to make such a circuit as would increase its length to two thousand feet.

Hence it is apparent that the ordinary road in a hilly and uneven country should follow the streams as far as possible, as Nature has located them in the places best adapted for highways; and when hills are found on the line of a road they should be surmounted by passing around and across them at the easiest grades possible rather than over them at steep grades.

CHAPTER III
CONSTRUCTION

Suitable drainage is the first requisite of a good road, as with our climate and soil it is impossible to have a road in a satisfactory condition at all seasons of the year unless the same is well drained. In building a new road provisions should be made to get rid of all surface water, and in wet land of the water in the soil, by ditches and drains sufficient to dispose of it in a thorough manner; and in repairing an old road it frequently happens that its condition can be greatly improved and sometimes perfected by simply providing proper drainage for it. It is not sufficient to have ditches on each side of the road; for if the water stands in them it is liable to make the road muddy and to weaken its substratum. The ditches themselves should be thoroughly drained, and all the water which accumulates in them should be carried into the natural watercourses of the country, or at any rate beyond the limits of the highway.

Every carriage-road ought to be wide enough at nearly all points to allow two vehicles to pass each other in safety. Whether it should be wider than that depends upon its location and its importance as a public thoroughfare. Any unnecessary width should be avoided, except on pleasure and showy boulevards, because thereby land is wasted, and labor and cost in construction and repair are increased. All important highways should be wide enough to admit of footpaths five or six feet wide on each side, and of a macadamized or travelled way commensurate to the public traffic thereon.

If a road is to be made wider than two vehicles require, it should be made wide enough to accommodate one or more vehicles; for any intermediate width causes unequal and excessive wear, and therefore is false economy.

The road-bed should generally be raised above the level of the surrounding land, in order that it may be as free as possible from water; and it should "crown" sufficiently to allow all the surface water, to find its way quickly into the side ditches. If it is not crowned enough, it soon becomes hollow, and therefore either muddy or dusty, and in times of heavy rains or thaws the water stands or flows in the middle of the road. If it is crowned too much, the drivers of vehicles will seek the middle of the road in order to keep their vehicles in level positions, and consequently the excessive travel in one part of the road soon wears it into ruts in which water accumulates, and carriages in meeting are forced to travel on a side hill, which causes unnecessary wear to the road by sliding down towards the ditches. This sliding tendency greatly augments the labor of the horses and the wear and tear of the carriages. Evidently, then, the wise course to pursue in the matter of crowning the road is to hit the golden mean. Much of success in life depends upon striking the golden mean, for human experience teaches that those who follow in this pathway are apt to find themselves among the happy and the successful. The advice which the wise old Horace made a sage seaman give two thousand years ago is good for road-makers of to-day,—

> "Licinius, trust a seaman's lore:
> Steer not too boldly to the deep;
> Nor dreading storms by treacherous shore
> Too closely creep."

It ought therefore to be an accepted maxim in road-making that the road-bed should be so constructed as to induce vehicles to travel it equally in every part.

For our climate and soil, no doubt, a macadamized road is the cheapest and best for general travel. This is made by covering the bottom of the road-bed with stones broken into angular pieces to a depth of from four to twelve inches. The bottom of the road-bed should be solid earth, and crowned sufficiently to carry off all water that may reach it. The depth of the stone coating may properly vary from four to twelve inches, as required by the nature of the soil, the climate, and the travel on it; and the size of the broken stones may also be varied to meet the requirements of the road. If there is to be heavy travel on the road, the stone coating should be thicker than on a road over which only lightly loaded teams are expected to pass; and in the former case the broken stones should be larger than in the latter case. In any event, the top of the stone coating should be composed of stones broken into small fragments. A coating, from four to six inches in depth, of broken stones from one to two inches in diameter is ordinarily sufficient to make a hard, dry, and beautiful country-road, if kept up at all seasons of the year. Flat or round stones should never be used, because they will not unite and consolidate into a mass, as small angular stones will do. When travel is first admitted upon the stone coating, the ruts should be filled up as soon as formed; or what is better, a heavy roller should be used until the stones have become well consolidated.

Sometimes in wet or clayey soil it is well to put at the bottom of the stone coating a layer of large stones, set on their broadest edges and lengthwise across the road in the form of a pavement. This is called a Telford road, and has advantages over the McAdam road in a soil retentive of moisture, as the layer of large stones operates as an under drain to the stone coating above it.

It is undoubtedly true that the McAdam or Telford road is the best road for all practical purposes in this country, and will be the country road of the future; yet it is also true that the most of our highways are mere earth-roads, and will probably remain such for many years, and it is therefore desirable that they should be constructed as well as they can be made. It is an admitted canon of the road-making art, that a road ought to be so hard and smooth that wheels will roll easily over it and not sink into it, so dry and compact that rain will not affect it beyond making it dirty, and its component parts so firmly moulded together that the sun cannot convert them into deep dust. Therefore the travelled part of an earth-road should not be composed of loam fertile enough for a corn-field, nor of sand deep enough for a beach. If the road runs through sandy land, it can be greatly and cheaply improved by covering it with a few inches of clayish soil; and if it runs through clayey land, a similar application of sand will be beneficial. A gravelly soil is usually the best material for an earth-road, and when practicable every such road should be covered with a coating of it. The larger gravel, however, should never be placed at the bottom and the smaller at the top, as the frost and the vehicles will cause the large gravel to rise and the small to descend, like the materials in a shaken sieve, and the road will never become smooth and hard.

CHAPTER IV
REPAIRS

After a road is located and constructed, economy as well as public convenience demands that it be kept in good condition the year round. If a road is allowed to go for several months at a time without repairs, ruts and holes are likely to form on its surface, and frequently the middle becomes lower than the sides. Then, in order to put it in good condition again, a great deal of work and expense are necessary, whereas if every break is repaired immediately, much less labor and expense are required to keep up the road for the same length of time, besides the increased advantage and convenience of a good road from day to day.

No doubt our roads could be kept in better condition than at present without any additional expense, by the application of good sense and business principles in their management. The present system in nearly all our country towns consists in dividing up the roads into districts, and appointing a highway surveyor for each district, with a stated allowance of money to expend on repairs; and sometimes the tax-payer residing in the district has a right to work out his road tax. This surveyor is usually a farmer, who is very busy during planting-time in the spring, and during the haying and harvesting seasons; and consequently he works upon the roads between the planting and the haying seasons, or in the autumn after he has finished the fall work upon his farm. It sometimes happens that he works out all the money allowed him in early summer, and then nothing more is done for a year.

If a road is only to be repaired once a year, the work ought to be done in the spring, when the soil is moist and will pack together hard, and not in the summer, when it is dry and turns easily to dust, nor in the late autumn, when the fall rains make it muddy. The surveyor generally makes the repairs by ploughing up the road-bed and smoothing it off a little, or else by ploughing up the dust, turf, and stones alongside the road-bed, and scraping the same upon it. After this is done he goes about his farm work.

The stones in the road soon begin to work up to the surface, and remain there like so many footballs for every horse to kick as he passes over them.

A horse-path naturally forms in the centre of the road, and wheel-ruts upon either side, which make excellent channels for the water to run in during every rain-storm. At first the water finds its way over the water-bars in small quantities; but the channels increase in depth with every shower, and soon during every hard rain there are from one to three streams of water running over the road-bed from the top to the bottom of nearly every hill, and as a consequence the road is washed all to pieces. The road then generally remains in this condition until the next fall, and sometimes until the next spring. When a road is repaired in this way, it follows as a matter of course that it is in a bad condition all the year round. Just after repairs the road is wretched, for it is then in better condition to be planted than to be travelled over; when trodden down a little, the wash of the rains and the loose stones make it bad again; it then grows worse and worse until another general repair makes it wretched again, and so on *ad infinitum*. The only way to remedy this state of affairs is to change the system.

There should be only one highway surveyor for the whole town, with authority to supply such men and teams as may be necessary to keep the roads in a good state of repair. Let them not only work in the early summer and fall, but at all times when there is anything which needs to be done to the roads. A few shovels of dirt and a little labor in the nick of time will do more towards keeping a road in good condition than whole days of ploughing and scraping once or twice a year only. Every good housewife knows that there is a world of truth in the old maxim, "A stitch in time saves nine." The managers of all our well-conducted railroads understand this. They have a gang of men pass often over each section of the roads.

What would be said of a mill-owner who should let his milldam wash away once or twice each year, and then rebuild it instead of keeping it in constant repair? The proprietors of the great turnpike road from Sacramento to Virginia City in California, which runs mainly over mountains a distance of one hundred and fifty miles, and has an annual traffic of seven or eight thousand heavy teams, have found by careful experiment that the cheapest way to keep that great road in good condition is to have every portion of it looked after every day, and during dry weather every rod of it is sprinkled with water. This continual-repair system was adopted in Baden, Germany, 1845. It was soon found that it was less expensive and more satisfactory than the old system of annual repairs. Other European countries soon found it to their advantage to follow Baden's example in this respect; and now the new system is in universal use in all the civilized nations of Europe. As a consequence the roads in those countries as a general thing are in splendid condition throughout the year. They are on an even grade, and as smooth as a racing-track in this country. The poorest roads in France, Germany,

Switzerland, or Great Britain are as good as the best of our own. They are nearly all macadamized, and are kept in continuous repair by laborers and competent engineers and surveyors, who give their sole labor and attention to the roads as a business throughout the year.

But it is not necessary to go to Europe to prove the superiority of the new system over the old. Many towns in this country, especially those situated in the vicinity of the large cities, have adopted the new system, and find by experiment that it is better than the old. An intelligent citizen and town official of Chelmsford, Mass., Mr. Henry S. Perham, thus describes the operation of the old and the new system in that town: "Until 1877 the old highway district system, common in the New England country towns, was in vogue here. Eleven highway surveyors were chosen annually in town-meeting, who had charge of the roads in their respective districts; and although the town appropriated money liberally for highway repairs, the roads seemed to be continually growing worse, owing to the superficial manner in which the repairs were made. In 1877 the town adopted an entirely different plan for doing the work. The plan was to choose one surveyor for the whole town, who was to have charge of all the roads, and the town to purchase suitable teams and implements to be kept at the town farm. This is now the ninth year in which this system has been in practice, and the result of the change has been most satisfactory. The advantages are that the surveyor is chosen for his especial fitness for the work. The men under him are mostly employed by the month and boarded at the town farm, where the teams are also kept. A force now costing the town ten dollars per day will accomplish more and better work in one week than would be ordinarily accomplished by a surveyor under the old system in a season. And the reason is obvious. The men and teams are accustomed to the work; the best implements and machinery are employed, road-scrapers doing the work where the nature of the soil will permit; and what is still more important, the work is directed by the surveyor to the best advantage. In the winter season the teams break out the roads after heavy snows, and in fair weather cart gravel on to the roads as in summer. And although we have an extraordinary length of road to support,—namely, two hundred and seventy-five miles, being more by twenty-five miles than any other town in the State,—there has been a marked and continual improvement in their condition.

"When this plan was first presented to the attention of the town, it met with sharp opposition, and passed by only a small majority; but the favor with which it is now regarded may be judged by the fact that since its adoption it has met with almost universal approval, and we should now as soon think of going back to the school-district system or to support the churches by taxation as of returning to the old method of repairing our roads."

This method is undoubtedly better than the old district system; but the system of the future will not include a road-scraper except for the building of new roads. Any system is radically defective which scrapes the dust and worn-out soil of the gutters or the turf and loam of the roadside upon the road-bed. Perhaps this kind of repairing is better than none in many localities; but as civilization advances and the true principles of road-making become better known, after the foundation of a road-bed has been properly established, nothing but good road material will ever be put upon it, and this will be put there from time to time as needed to keep up a continual good condition of the road.

CHAPTER V
LAWS RELATING TO THE LAYING OUT OF WAYS

New roads are not often required now to reach and develop new tracts of land, except in large towns and cities; but they are frequently needed to shorten distances and to improve grades. Consequently the laws relative to the laying out, maintenance, and use of highways are of personal interest to every citizen, and many are also interested in the laws relating to private ways.

The public have a right to lay out ways for purposes of business, amusement, or recreation, as to markets, to public parks or commons, to places of historic interest or beautiful natural scenery.1 And such ways may be established by prescription, by dedication, or by the acts of the proper public authorities. Twenty years' uninterrupted use by the public will make a prescriptive highway. Many of the old roads in our towns and cities have become public thoroughfares by prescriptive use, which began in colonial days, and perhaps then followed Indian trails, or were first used as bridle-paths.

When the owner in fee of land gives to the public a right of passage and repassage over it, and his gift is accepted by the public, the land thus travelled over becomes a way by dedication. The dedication may be made by the writing, the declaration, or by the acts of the owner. It must, however, clearly appear that he intended and has made the dedication; and when it has been accepted by the public it is irrevocable. Formerly it could be accepted by the public by use, or by some act or circumstance showing the town's assent and acquiescence in such dedication; but now no city or town is chargeable for such dedicated way until it has been laid out and established in the manner provided by the statutes.2 It was formerly thought that this act applied to prescriptive ways as well as to dedicated ways; but it is now settled that it applies only to ways by dedication, and ways by prescription are not affected by it.3

The proper town or city authorities have jurisdiction to lay out or alter ways within the limits of their respective cities or towns, and to order specific repairs thereon. The county commissioners have also jurisdiction to lay out public ways, the termini of which are exclusively within the same town; and they are also clothed with authority to lay them out from town to town. Hence roads may be either town ways or public highways. When the proceedings for their location originate with the town or city officials, they are town ways; and when the proceedings originate with the county commissioners, they are public highways.4 Suppose a new road is wanted, or an alteration in an old one is desired, within the limits of a town, a petition therefor may be presented either to the town authorities or to the county commissioners. If the proposed road is not situated entirely within the limits of one town or city, then the commissioners alone have jurisdiction in the premises. When the selectmen or road commissioners of a town decide to lay out a new road, or to alter an old one, their doings must be reported and allowed at some public meeting of the inhabitants regularly warned and notified therefor; but while the inhabitants are vested with the right of approval, they have no right to vote that the selectmen or road commissioners shall lay out a particular way, as it is the intention of the statute that these officials shall exercise their own discretion upon the subject.5 If the town authorities unreasonably refuse or neglect to lay out a way, or if the town unreasonably refuses or delays to approve and allow such way as laid out or altered by its officials, then the parties aggrieved thereby may, at any time within one year, apply to the county commissioners, who have authority to cause such way to be laid out or altered. But when a petition for a public way is presented in the first instance to the county commissioners, or when the matter is brought before them by way of appeal, their decision on the question of the public necessity and convenience of such way is final, and from it there is no appeal. If damage is sustained by any person in his property by the laying out, alteration, or discontinuance of a public way, he is entitled to receive just and adequate damages therefor, to be assessed, in the first place, by the town or city authorities or by the county commissioners, and, finally, by a jury, in case one is demanded by him. He is entitled to a reasonable time to take off any timber, wood or trees, which may be upon the land to be taken; but if he does not remove the same within the time allowed, he is deemed to have relinquished his right thereto. In estimating the damage to the land-owner caused by the laying out or the alteration of a public way over his land, neither the city nor town authorities nor a jury are confined to the value of the land taken. He is also entitled to the amount of the damage done to his remaining land by such laying out or alteration.6 But in such estimation of damages any direct or peculiar benefit or increase of value accruing to his adjoining land is to be allowed as a betterment, by way of set-off; but not any general benefit or increase of value received by him in common with other land in the neighborhood.7

The cost of making and altering ways, including damages caused thereby, is to be paid by the city or town wherein the same are located, provided the proceedings originate with the town or city authorities; but when the proceedings originate with the county commissioners, they divide the cost between the towns and the county in such manner as they think to be just and reasonable.8

CHAPTER VI
LAW AS TO REPAIRS

After highways, town-ways, streets, causeways, and bridges have been established, they are to be kept in such repair as to be reasonably safe and convenient for travellers at all seasons of the year at the expense of the town or city in which they are situated.

It is the duty of each town to grant and vote such sums of money as are necessary for repairing the public ways within its borders; and if it fails to do so, the highway surveyors, in their respective districts, may employ persons, as directed in the statutes, to repair the roads, and the persons so employed may collect pay for their labor of the town. In order to make such repairs, city and town authorities may select and lay out land within their respective limits as gravel and clay pits from which may be taken earth and gravel necessary for the construction and repairs of streets and ways.9 And they may turn the surface drainage of the roads upon the land of the adjoining owners without liability.10 But no highway surveyor has a right, without the written approbation of the selectmen, to cause a watercourse, occasioned by the wash of the road, to be so conveyed by the roadside as to incommode a house, a store, shop, or other building, or to obstruct a person in the prosecution of his business.11 Properly authorized city or town officers may trim or lop off trees and bushes standing in the public ways, or cut down and remove such trees; and may cause to be dug up and removed whatever obstructs such ways, or endangers, hinders, or incommodes persons travelling therein.12 Even the boundaries of public ways are so well guarded that when they are ascertainable no length of time less than forty years justifies the continuance of a fence or building within their limits; but the same may, upon the presentment of a grand jury, be removed as a nuisance.13

It is so important that the public ways be kept free for travel, that any person may take down and remove gates, rails, bars, or fences upon or across highways, unless the same have been there placed for the purpose of preventing the spreading of a disease dangerous to the public health, or have been erected or continued by the license of the selectmen or county commissioners.14 A highway surveyor acting within the scope of his authority may dig up and remove the soil within the limits of the public ways for the purpose of repairing the same, and may carry it from one part of the town to another;15 and he has a right to deposit the soil thus removed on his own land, if that is the best way of clearing the road of useless material.16

Though the law is imperative that the roads must be kept in good condition, and to this end gives municipal corporations great powers, yet let no one who is not a highway surveyor or in his employ imagine that he can repair a road not on his own land with impunity; for it has been decided that if an unauthorized person digs up the soil on the roadside by another person's land for the purpose of repairing the road, he is a trespasser and liable for damages, although he does only what a highway surveyor might properly do.17 It is also the duty of cities and towns to guard with sufficient and suitable railings every road which passes over a bank, bridge, or along a precipice, excavation, or deep water; and it makes no difference whether these dangerous places are within or without the limits of the road, if they are so imminent to the line of public travel as to expose travellers to unusual hazard.18 But towns are not obliged to put up railings merely to prevent travellers from straying out of the highway, where there is no unsafe place immediately contiguous to the way.19

The roads are for the use of travellers, and a city or town is not bound to keep up railings strong enough for idlers to lounge against or children to play upon.20

The travelled parts of all roads ought to be wide enough to allow of the ordinary shyings and frights of horses with safety, for shying is one of the natural habits of the animal;21 although it seems that switching his tail over the reins is not a natural habit of the animal, as it has been decided that if a horse throws his tail over the reins and thereby a defect in the road is run against, no damages can be recovered.22

CHAPTER VII
GUIDE-POSTS, DRINKING-TROUGHS, AND FOUNTAINS

The statutes undertake to provide for the erection and maintenance of guide-posts at suitable places on the public ways; but a person has to travel but little in many of the towns of the State to come to the conclusion that the law is either deficient in construction or a dead letter in execution. The law makes it incumbent upon the selectmen or road commissioners of each town to submit to the inhabitants, at every annual meeting, a report of all the places in which guide-posts are erected and maintained within the town, and of all places at which, in their opinion, they ought to be erected and maintained. For each neglect or refusal to make such report they shall severally forfeit ten dollars. After the report is made the town shall determine the several places at which guide-posts shall be erected and maintained, which shall be recorded in the town records. A town which neglects or refuses to determine such places, and to cause a record thereof to be made, shall forfeit five dollars for every month during which it neglects or refuses to do so.

At each of the places determined by the town there shall be erected, unless the town at the annual meeting agrees upon some suitable substitute therefor, a substantial post of not less than eight feet in height, near the upper end of which shall be placed a board or boards, with plain inscription thereon, directing travellers to the next town or towns and informing them of the distance thereto.

Every town which neglects or refuses to erect and maintain such guide-posts, or some suitable substitutes therefor, shall forfeit annually five dollars for every guide-post which it neglects or refuses to maintain.23 These forfeitures can be recovered either by indictment or by an action of tort for the benefit of the county wherein the acts of negligence or refusal occur; and any interested or public-spirited person can make complaint of such negligence or refusal to the superior court, or to any trial justice, police, district or municipal court, having jurisdiction of the matter.24

The selectmen may establish and maintain such drinking-troughs, wells, and fountains within the public highways, squares, and commons of their respective towns, as in their judgment the public necessity and convenience may require, and the towns may vote money to defray the expenses thereof.25 But the vote of a town instructing the selectmen to establish a watering-trough at a particular place would be irregular and void, because towns in their corporate capacity have not been given the right by statute to construct drinking-troughs in the public highways. And towns would not be liable for the acts of the selectmen performed in pursuance of this statute, because the law makes the selectmen a board of public officers, representing the general public, and not the agents of their respective towns. However, if the inhabitants of a town should construct a drinking trough or fountain of such hideous shape, and paint it with such brilliant color, that it would frighten an ordinarily gentle and well-broken horse, by reason of which a traveller should be brought in contact with a defect in the way or on the side of the way, and thus injured, the town might be held liable to pay damages.26

It is my purpose to state what the law is, and not what it ought to be; but I will venture the suggestion that it would not be an unreasonable hardship on towns to require them to establish and maintain suitable watering-troughs at suitable places, and it would be a merciful kindness to many horses which now frequently have to travel long distances over dusty roads in summer heat without a chance to get a swallow of water from a public drinking-trough.

CHAPTER VIII
SHADE TREES, PARKS, AND COMMONS

The law of the Commonwealth not only requires the public ways to be kept safe and convenient, but of late years statutes have been passed allowing owners of land, improvement societies, cities and towns, to do something to beautify the roadsides and public squares of any city or town. A city or town may grant or vote a sum not exceeding fifty cents for each of its ratable polls in the preceding year, to be expended in planting, or encouraging the planting by the owners of adjoining real estate, of shade trees upon the public squares or highways.27 Such trees may be planted wherever it will not interfere with the public travel or with private rights, and they shall be deemed and taken to be the private property of the person so planting them or upon whose premises they stand.28

Improvement societies, properly organized for the purpose of improving and ornamenting the streets and public squares of any city or town by planting and cultivating ornamental trees therein, may be authorized by any town to use, take care of, and control the public grounds or open spaces in any of its public ways, not needed for public travel. They may grade, drain, curb, set out shade or ornamental trees, lay out flower plots, and otherwise improve the same; and may protect their work by suitable fences or railings, subject to such directions as may be given by the selectmen or road commissioners. And any person who wantonly, maliciously, or mischievously drives cattle, horses, or other animals, or drives teams, carriages, or other vehicles, on or across such grounds or open spaces, or removes or destroys any fence or railing on the same, or plays ball or other games thereon, or otherwise interferes with or damages the work of such corporation, is subject to a fine not exceeding twenty dollars for each offence, for the benefit of the society.29

It is also a legal offence for any one wantonly to injure or deface a shade tree, shrub, rose, or other plant or fixture of ornament or utility in a street, road, square, court, park, or public garden, or carelessly to suffer a horse or other beast driven by or for him, or a beast belonging to him and lawfully on the highway, to break down or injure a tree, not his own, standing for use or ornament on said highway.30 And no one, even if he be the owner of the land, has the right to cut down or remove an ornamental or shade tree standing in a public way, without first giving notice of his intention to the municipal authorities, who are entitled to ten days to decide whether the tree can be removed or not. And whoever cuts down or removes or injures such tree in violation of the law shall forfeit not less than five nor more than one hundred dollars for the benefit of the city or town wherein the same stands.31

CHAPTER IX
PUBLIC USE OF HIGHWAYS

After the roads are ready for use and beautified by shade trees and green parks at convenient places, we are confronted with the question, How are they to be used by the public and the owners of adjoining estates? We, as a people, are not only continental and terrestrial travellers, but we are continually passing hither and thither over the public ways of this State, and consequently it is important for us to know how to travel the common roads in a legal and proper manner.

In the first place, every one who travels upon a public thoroughfare is bound to drive with due care and discretion, and to have an ordinarily gentle and well trained horse, with harness and vehicle in good roadworthy condition, as he is liable for whatever damages may be occasioned by any insufficiency in this respect.32

Another duty which every traveller is bound to observe is to drive at a moderate rate of speed. To drive a carriage or other vehicle on a public way at such a rate or in such a manner as to endanger the safety of other travellers, or the inhabitants along the road, is an indictable offence at common law, and amounts to a breach of the peace; and in case any one is injured or damaged thereby, he may look to the fast driver for his recompense. But it does not follow that a man may not drive a well-bred and high-spirited horse at a rapid gait, if he does not thereby violate any ordinance or by-law of a town or city; for it has been held that it cannot be said, as matter of law, that a man is negligent who drives a high-spirited and lively-stepping horse at the rate of ten miles an hour in a dark night.33

It then behooves every one to drive with care and caution, whether he is going fast or slow; and it also behooves him to see that his servants drive with equal care and caution, for he is responsible to third persons for the negligence of his servants, in the scope of their employment, to the same extent as if the act were his own, although the servants disobey his express orders. If you send your servant upon the road with a team, with instructions to drive carefully and to avoid coming in contact with any carriage, but instead of driving carefully he drives carelessly against a carriage, you are liable for all damages resulting from the collision; and if the servant acts wantonly or mischievously, causing thereby additional bodily or mental injury, such wantonness or mischief will enhance the damage against you.34

You may think this a hard law; but it is not so hard as it would be if it allowed you to hire ignorant, wilful, and incompetent servants to go upon the road and injure the lives and property of innocent people without redress save against the servants, who perchance might be financially irresponsible. It should however be stated in this connection that if your team should get away from you or your servant, without any fault on your or his part, and should run away and do great damage, by colliding with other teams, or by running over people on foot, you would not be held responsible, as in law it would be regarded as an inevitable accident. Thus, if your horse should get scared by some sudden noise or frightful object by the wayside, or through his natural viciousness of which you were ignorant, or by some means should get unhitched after you had left him securely tied, and in consequence thereof should plunge the shaft of your wagon into some other man's horse, or should knock down and injure a dozen people, you would not be liable, because the injury resulted from circumstances over which you had no control.35

CHAPTER X
"THE LAW OF THE ROAD"

There are certain rules applicable to travellers upon public ways, which are so important that everybody ought to know and observe them. The law relative thereto is known as "the law of the road." These rules relate to the meeting, passing, and conduct of teams on the road; and it is more important that there should be some well established and understood rules on the subject than what the rules are. In England the rules are somewhat different, and some of them are the reverse of what they are in this country. But the rules and the law relating thereto in this country are about the same in every State of the Union. Our statutes provide that when persons meet each other on a bridge or road, travelling with carriages or other vehicles, each person shall seasonably drive his carriage or other vehicle to the right of the middle of the travelled part of such bridge or road, so that their respective carriages or other vehicles may pass each other without interference; that one party passing another going in the same direction must do so on the left-hand side of the middle of the road, and if there is room enough, the foremost driver must not wilfully obstruct the road.36

Although these are statutory rules, yet they are not inflexible in every instance, as on proper occasions they may be waived or reversed. They are intended for the use of an intelligent and civilized people; and in the crowded streets of villages and cities, situations or circumstances may frequently arise when a deviation will not only be justifiable but absolutely necessary. One may always pass on the left side of a road, or across it, for the purpose of stopping on that side, if he can do so without interrupting or obstructing a person lawfully passing on the other side.37 And if the driver of a carriage on the proper side of the road sees a horse coming furiously on the wrong side of the road, it is his duty to give way and go upon the wrong side of the road, if by so doing he can avoid an accident.38 But in deviating from the "law of the road," one must be able to show that it was the proper and reasonable thing to do under the circumstances, or else he will be answerable for all damages; for the law presumes that a party who is violating an established rule of travelling is a wrongdoer.39 Of course a person on the right side of the road has no right to run purposely or recklessly into a trespasser, simply because he has wrongfully given him the opportunity to receive an injury, and then turn round and sue for damages arising from his own foolhardiness and devil-may-care conduct.40

Every one seeking redress at law on account of an accident must be able to show that he himself was at the time in the exercise of ordinary care and precaution, and it is not enough for him to show that somebody else was violating a rule of law. When the road is unoccupied a traveller is at liberty to take whichever side of the road best suits his convenience, as he is only required "seasonably to drive to the right" when he meets another traveller; but if parties meet *on the sudden*, and an injury results, the party on the wrong side of the road is responsible, unless it clearly appears that the party on the proper side has ample means and opportunity to prevent it.41

Where there is occasion for one driver to pass another going in the same direction, the foremost driver may keep the even tenor of his way in the middle or on either side of the road, provided there is sufficient room for the rear driver to pass by; but if there is not sufficient room, it is the duty of the foremost driver to afford it, by yielding an equal share of the road, if that be practicable; but if not, then the object must be deferred till the parties arrive at ground more favorable to its accomplishment. If the leading traveller then wilfully refuses to comply, he makes himself liable, criminally, to the penalty imposed by the statute, and answerable at law in case the rear traveller suffers damage in consequence of the delay. There being no statute regulations as to the manner in which persons should drive when they meet at the junction of two streets, the rule of the common law applies, and each person is bound to use due and reasonable care, adapted to the circumstances and place.42

By the "travelled part" of the road is intended that part which is usually wrought for travelling, and not any track which may happen to be made in the road by the passing of vehicles; but when the wrought part of the road is hidden by the snow, and a path is beaten and travelled on the side of the wrought part, persons meeting on such beaten and travelled path are required to drive their vehicles to the right of the middle of such path.43 Many drivers of heavily loaded vehicles seem to think that all lightly loaded ones should turn out and give them all the travelled part of the road. No doubt a lightly loaded vehicle can often turn out with less inconvenience than a heavily loaded one, and generally every thoughtful and considerate driver of a light vehicle is willing to, and does, give the heavy vehicle more than half the road on every proper occasion; but the driver of the heavy vehicle ought to understand that it is done out of courtesy to himself and consideration for his horses, and not because it is required by any rule of law. The statute law of the road in this State makes no distinction between the lightly and the heavily loaded vehicle. Both alike are required to pass to the right of the travelled part of the road. In case of accident the court would undoubtedly take into consideration the size and load of each vehicle, as bearing upon the question of the conduct of the drivers under the circumstances, and their responsibility would be settled in accordance with "the law of the road," modified and possibly reversed by the situation of the parties and the circumstances surrounding them at the time.44

A traveller in a common carriage may use the track of a street railway when the same is not in use by the company; but the company is entitled to the unrestricted use of their rails upon all proper occasions, and then such traveller must keep off their track, or else he renders himself liable to indictment under the statutes of the State.45

CHAPTER XI
EQUESTRIANS AND PEDESTRIANS

In England "the law of the road" applies as well to equestrians as to travellers by carriage, and I can see no good reason why it should not do so here. The statutes are silent on the subject, and I cannot find that our Supreme Court has ever had occasion to pass upon the question; but it has been decided in some of the States that when a traveller on horseback meets another equestrian or a carriage, he may exercise his own notions of prudence, and turn either to the right or to the left at his option.46 By common consent and immemorial usage an equestrian is expected to yield the road, or a good share of it, to a wagon or other vehicle. It has been decided in Pennsylvania that if he has a chance to turn out and refuses to do so, and his steed or himself is injured by a collision, he is remediless.47

It is clear that the statute law of the road in this State is not applicable to people on horseback, as it is expressly limited to carriages or other vehicles, and therefore equestrians are amenable only to the common law of the land. By this law they are required to ride on the public ways with due care and precaution, and to exercise reasonably good judgment on every occasion, under all the attendant circumstances. When they meet wagons, whether heavily loaded or not, they ought to yield as much of the road as they can conveniently,—certainly more than half, as they do not need that much of the road to pass conveniently,—but when they meet a vehicle in the form of a bicycle there seems to be no good reason why they should yield more than half the road. For the convenience of themselves and the public at large, on meeting vehicles or each other, they ought to pass to the right, as by adopting the statute law of the road in this respect order is promoted and confusion avoided.

A public thoroughfare is a way for foot-passengers as well as carriages, and a person has a right to walk on the carriage-way if he pleases; but, as Chief Justice Denman once remarked, "he had better not, especially at night, when carriages are passing along."48 However, all persons have an undoubted right to walk on the beaten track of a road, if it has no sidewalk, even if infirm with age or disease, and are entitled to the exercise of reasonable care on the part of persons driving vehicles along it. If there is a sidewalk which is in bad condition, or obstructed by merchandise or otherwise, then the foot-passenger has a right to walk on the road if he pleases. But it should be borne in mind that what is proper on a country road might not be in the crowded streets of a city. In law every one is bound to regulate his conduct to meet the situations in which he is placed, and the circumstances around him at the time. A person infirm with age or disease or afflicted with poor eyesight should always take extraordinary precaution in walking upon the road.49 Thus, a man who traverses a crowded thoroughfare with edged tools or bars of iron must take especial care that he does not cut or bruise others with the things he carries. Such a person would be bound to keep a better lookout than the man who merely carried an umbrella; and the man who carried an umbrella would be bound to take more care when walking with it than a person who had nothing.50

Footmen have a right to cross a highway on every proper occasion, but when convenient they should pass upon cross-walks, and in so doing should look out for teams; for it is as much their duty, on crossing a road, to look out for teams, as it is the duty of the drivers of teams to be vigilant in not running over them. "The law of the road" as to the meeting of vehicles does not apply to them. They may walk upon whichever side they please, and turn, upon meeting teams, either to the right or to the left, at their option, but it is their duty to yield the road to such an extent as is necessary and reasonable; and if they walk in the beaten track or cross it when teams are passing along, they must use extraordinary care and caution or they will be remediless in case of injury to themselves. They may travel on the Lord's day for all purposes of necessity or charity; and they may also take short walks in the public highway on Sundays, simply for exercise and to take the air, and even to call to see friends on such walks, without liability to punishment therefor under the statutes for the observance of the Lord's day, and they can recover damages for injuries wrongfully sustained while so walking.51

CHAPTER XII
OMNIBUSES, STAGES, AND HORSE-CARS

Nearly every one has occasion, more or less often, to travel over the public ways in the coaches of passenger carriers. Whoever undertakes to carry passengers and their baggage for hire from place to place is bound to use the utmost care and diligence in providing safe and suitable coaches, harnesses, horses, and coachmen, in order to prevent such injuries as human care and foresight can guard against.

If an accident happens from a defect in the coach or harness which might have been discovered and remedied upon careful and thorough examination, such accident must be ascribed to negligence, for which the owner is liable in case of injury to a passenger happening by reason of such accident.

On the other hand, where the accident arises from a hidden and internal defect, which careful and thorough examination would not disclose, and which could not be guarded against by the exercise of sound judgment and the most vigilant oversight, then the proprietor is not liable for the injury, but the misfortune must be borne by the sufferer as one of that class of injuries for which the law can afford no redress in the form of a pecuniary recompense.

If a passenger, in peril arising from an accident for which the proprietors are responsible, is in so dangerous a situation as to render his leaping from the coach an act of reasonable precaution, and he leaps therefrom and breaks a limb, the proprietors are answerable to him in damages, though he might safely have retained his seat.52

When the proprietors of stages or street-car coaches, which are already full and overloaded, stop their coaches, whether at the signal or not of would-be passengers, and open the doors for their entrance, they must be considered as inviting them to ride, and thereby assuring them that their passage will be a safe one, at least so far as dependent upon the exercise of reasonable and ordinary care, diligence, and skill, on their part, in driving and managing their horses and coaches; and, in fact, they are rather to be held responsible for such increased watchfulness and solicitous care, skill, and attention, as the crowded condition of the vehicle requires. If, under such circumstances, a passenger is thrown out of or off the coach by its violent jerk at starting or stopping, or in any other way through the negligence of the proprietors or their agents, he may hold them liable for his injuries.53 A passenger must pay his fare in advance, if demanded, otherwise he may have to pay a fine for evading fare; and if he is riding free, the proprietors are not responsible, except for gross negligence; and he must also properly and securely pack his baggage, if he expects to recover damages in case of loss. A mail-coach is protected by act of Congress from obstructions, but is subject in all other respects to "the law of the road."54

If the proprietors of coaches used for the common carriage of persons are guilty of gross carelessness or neglect in the conduct and management of the same while in such use, they are liable to a fine not exceeding five thousand dollars, or to imprisonment not exceeding three years.55 And if a driver of a stage-coach or other vehicle for the conveyance of passengers for hire, when a passenger is within or upon such coach or vehicle, leaves the horses thereof without some suitable person to take the charge and guidance of them, or without fastening them in a safe and prudent manner, he may be imprisoned two months or fined fifty dollars.56

CHAPTER XIII
PURPOSES FOR WHICH HIGHWAYS MAY BE USED

As before intimated, the public ways are mainly for the use of travellers; but in the progress of civilization it has become convenient and necessary to use them for other purposes of a public nature. It is the great merit of the common law, that while its fundamental principles remain fixed from generation to generation, yet they are generally so comprehensive and so well adapted to new institutions and conditions of society, new modes of commerce, new usages and practices, that they are capable of application to every phase of society and business life. Time and necessity, as well as locality, are important elements in determining the character of any particular use of a public way. Many public ways are now used for gas, water-pipes, and sewers, because the public health and convenience are subserved by such use.57 They are also used for the transmission of intelligence by electricity, and the post-boy and the mail-coach are disappearing.

The horse-railroad was deemed a new invention; but it was held that a portion of the road might well be set aside for it, although the rights of other travellers to some extent were limited by the privileges necessary for its use.58

And now motor cars and elevated railroads are making their appearance in the centres of civilized life, and the bicycle and tricycle are familiar objects on all the great thoroughfares. Should human ingenuity discover any new modes of conveying persons and property over the public ways, or of transmitting intelligence along the same, which should prove convenient to the everyday life of humanity, no doubt the highway law will be found applicable to all the needs of advancing civilization. The underlying principle of the law is that every person may use the highway to his own best advantage, but with a just regard to the like rights of others. The law does not specify what kind of animals or vehicles are to be allowed upon the road, but leaves every case to be decided as it shall arise, in view of the customs and necessities of the people from time to time. All persons may lawfully travel upon the public ways with any animal or vehicle which is suitable for a way prepared and intended to afford the usual and reasonable accommodations needful to the requirements of a people in their present state of civilization; but if any person undertakes to use or travel upon the highway in an unusual or extraordinary manner, or with animals, vehicles, or freight not suitable or adapted to a way opened and prepared for the public use, in the common intercourse of society, and in the transaction of usual and ordinary business, he then takes every possible risk of loss and damage upon himself.59

If a party leads a bull or other animal through a public way without properly guarding and restraining the same, and for want of such care and restraint people rightfully on the way and using due care are injured, the owner of the animal is responsible, because under such circumstances he is bound to use the utmost care and diligence, especially in villages and cities, to avoid injuries to people on the road.60 So, if a man goes upon the highway with a vehicle of such peculiar and unusual construction, or which is operated in such a manner, as to frighten horses and to create noise and confusion on the road, he is guilty of an indictable offence and answerable in damages besides. An ycleped velocipede in the road has been held in Canada to be a nuisance, and its owner was indicted and found guilty of a criminal offence.61 In England a man who had taken a traction steam-engine upon the road was held liable to a party who had suffered damages by reason of his horses being frightened by it.62 It has been held to be a nuisance at common law to carry an unreasonable weight on a highway with an unusual number of horses.63 And so it is a nuisance for a large number of persons to assemble on or near a highway for the purpose of shouting and making a noise and disturbance; and likewise it is a nuisance for one to make a large collection of tubs in the road, or to blockade the way by a large number of logs, cattle, or wagons; for, as Lord Ellenborough once said, the king's highway is not to be used as a stable or lumber yard.

Towns and cities have authority to make such by-laws regulating the use and management of the public ways within their respective limits, not repugnant to law, as they shall judge to be most conducive to their welfare.64 They may make such by-laws to secure, among other things, the removal of snow and ice from sidewalks by the owners of adjoining estates; to prevent the pasturing of cattle or other animals in the highways; to regulate the driving of sheep, swine, and neat cattle over the public ways; to regulate the transportation of the offal of slaughtered cattle, sheep, hogs, and other animals along the roads; to prohibit fast driving or riding on the highways; to regulate travel over bridges; to regulate the passage of carriages or other vehicles, and sleds used for coasting, over the public ways; to regulate and control itinerant musicians who frequent the streets and public places; and to regulate the moving of buildings in the highways. Many people are inclined to make the highway the receptacle for the surplus stones and rubbish around their premises, and to use the wayside for a lumber and wood yard; and some farmers are in the habit of supplying their hog-pens and barn cellars with loam and soil dug out of the highway.

Again, some highway surveyors have very little taste for rural beauty, and show very poor judgment, and perhaps now and then a little spite, in ploughing up the green grass by the roadside and sometimes in front of houses. These evils can be remedied by every town which will pass suitable by-laws upon the subject and see that they are enforced. Such by-laws might provide that no one should be allowed to deposit within the limits of the highway any stones, brush, wood, rubbish, or other substance inconvenient to public travel; that no one should be permitted to dig up and carry away any loam or soil within the limits of the highway; and that no highway surveyor should be allowed to dig or plough up the greensward in front of any dwelling-house, or other building used in connection therewith, without the written direction or consent of the selectmen.

CHAPTER XIV
USE OF HIGHWAYS BY ADJOINING OWNERS

The owner of land adjoining a highway ordinarily owns to the middle of the road; and while he has the same rights as the public therein, he also has, in addition thereto, certain other rights incident to the ownership of the land over which the road passes. When land is taken for a highway, it is taken for all the present and prospective purposes for which a public thoroughfare may properly be used, and the damages to the owner of the land are estimated with reference to such use; but the land can be used for no other purpose, and when the servitude ceases the land reverts to him free from encumbrance. During the continuance of the servitude he is entitled to use the land, subject to the easement, for any and all purposes not incompatible with the public enjoyment. If the legislature authorizes the addition of any new servitude, essentially distinct from the ordinary use of a highway, like an elevated railroad, then the land-owner is entitled to additional compensation; for it cannot be deemed, in law, to have been within the contemplation of the parties, at the time of the laying out of the road, that it might be used for such new and additional purposes. It has been held in New York, Illinois, and some of the United States circuit courts, that the use of a highway for a telegraph line will entitle such owner to additional compensation; but in the recent case of Pierce *v.* Drew65 the majority of our Supreme Court decided that the erection of a telegraph line is not a new servitude for which the land-owner is entitled to additional compensation.

A minority of the court, in an able argument, maintained that the erection of telegraph and telephone posts and wires along the roads, fitted with cross-beams adapted for layer after layer of almost countless wires, which necessitate to some extent the destruction of trees along the highways or streets, the occupation of the ground, the filling of the air, the interference with access to or escape from buildings, the increased difficulty of putting out fires, the obstruction of the view, the presentation of unsightly objects to the eye, and the creation of unpleasant noises in the wind, is an actual injury to abutting land along the line, and constitutes a new and increased servitude, for which the land-owner is entitled to a distinct compensation. After the rendering of the majority decision, the legislature very promptly passed a law allowing an owner of land abutting upon a highway along which telegraph or telephone, electric light or electric power, lines shall be constructed, to recover damages to the full extent of the injuries to his property, provided he applies, within three months after such construction, to the mayor and aldermen or selectmen to assess and appraise his damage.66

The public has a right to occupy the highway for travel and other legitimate purposes, and to use the soil, the growing timber, and other materials found within the space of the road, in a reasonable manner, for the purpose of making and repairing the road and the bridges thereon.67 But the public cannot go upon the land of an adjoining owner without his consent, to remove stones or earth, to repair a bridge or the highway; and if in consequence of such removal the land is injured, by floods or otherwise, he can recover damages therefor.68 He is not obliged to build or maintain a road fence, except to keep his own animals at home, but if he does build a fence he must set it entirely on his own land; and likewise, if a town constructs an embankment to support a road or bridge, it must keep entirely within the limits of the highway, for if any part of the embankment is built on his land he can collect damages of the town.69 He may carry water-pipes underground through the highway, or turn a watercourse across the same below the surface, provided he does not deprive the public of their rights in the way.70 From the time of Edward IV. it has been the settled law that the owner of the soil in the highway is entitled to all the profits of the freehold, the grass and trees upon it and the mines under it. He can lawfully claim all the products of the soil and all the fruit and nuts upon the trees. He may maintain trespass for any injury to the soil or to the growing trees thereon, which is not incidental to the ordinary and legitimate uses of the road by the public. His land in the highway may be recovered in ejectment just the same as any of his other land. No one has any more right to graze his highway land than his tillage land.71 He may cut the hay on the roadside, gather the fruit and crops thereon, and graze his own animals there; and the by-laws of the cities and towns preventing the pasturing of cattle and other animals in the highway are not to affect his right to the use of land within the limits of the road adjoining his own premises.72

It is not one of the legitimate uses of the highway for a traveller or a loafer to stop in front of your house to abuse you with blackguardism, or to play a tune or sing a song which is objectionable to you; and if you request him to pass on and he refuses to go, you may treat him as a trespasser and make him pay damages and costs, if he is financially responsible.73 And likewise, if any person does anything on the highway in front of your premises to disturb the peace, to draw a crowd together, or to obstruct the way, he is answerable in damages to you and liable to an indictment by the grand jury.74

Although the owner of the fee in a highway has many rights in the way not common to the public, yet he must exercise those rights with due regard to the public safety and convenience. Perhaps, in the absence of objections on the part of the highway surveyor, or of prohibitory by-laws on the part of the town, he has a right to take soil or other material from the roadside for his own private use, but he certainly has no right to injure the road by his excavations, or to endanger the lives of travellers by leaving unsafe pits in the wayside. He can load and unload his vehicles in the highway, in connection with his business on the adjoining land, but it must be done in such a manner as not unreasonably to interfere with or incommode the travelling public. When a man finds it necessary to crowd his teams and wagons into the street, and thereby blockade the highway for hours at a time, he ought either to enlarge his premises or remove his business to some more convenient spot. He has a right to occupy the roadside with his vehicles, loaded or unloaded, to a reasonable extent; but when he fills up the road with logs and wood, tubs and barrels, wagons and sleighs, pig-pens and agricultural machinery, or deposits therein stones and rubbish, he is not using the highway properly, but is abusing it shamefully, and is responsible in damages to any one who is injured in person or property through his negligence, and, moreover, is liable to indictment for illegally obstructing the roadway.75 As before said, he has a perfect right to pasture the roadside with his animals; but if he turns them loose in the road, and they there injure the person or property of any one legally travelling therein, he is answerable in damages to the full extent of the injuries, whether he knows they have any vicious habits or not.76 If his cow, bull, or horse, thus loose in the highway, gore or kick the horse of some traveller, he is liable for all damages;77 and in one instance a peaceable and well-behaved hog in the road cost her owner a large sum of money, because the horse of a traveller, being frightened at her looks, ran away, smashed his carriage, and threw him out.78

As an offset to his advantages as adjoining owner there are a few disadvantages. Highways are set apart, among other things, that cattle and sheep may be driven thereon; and as, from the nature of such animals, it is impossible even with care to keep them upon the highways unless the adjoining land is properly fenced, it follows that when they are driven along the road with due care, and then escape upon adjoining land and do damage their owner is not liable therefor, if he makes reasonable efforts to remove them as speedily as possible.79 Likewise, if a traveller bent upon some errand of mercy or business finds the highway impassable by reason of some wash-out, snowdrift, or other defect, he may go round upon adjoining land, without liability, so far as necessary to bring him to the road again, beyond the defect.80 If a watercourse on adjoining land is allowed by the land-owner to become so obstructed by ice and snow, or other cause, that the water is set back, and overflows or obstructs the road, the highway surveyor may, without liability, enter upon adjoining land and remove the nuisance, if he acts with due regard to the safety and protection of the land from needless injury.81

A town or city has a right, in repairing a highway, to so raise the grade or so construct the water-bars within its limits, as to cause surface water to flow in large quantities upon adjoining land, to the injury of the owner thereof; but, on the other hand, the land-owner has a right to cause, if he can, the surface water on his land to flow off upon the highway, and he may lawfully do anything he can, on his own land, to prevent surface water from coming thereon from the highway, and may even stop up the mouth of a culvert built by a town across the way for the purpose of conducting such surface water upon his land, providing he can do it without exceeding the limits of his own land.82

When the owner of land is constructing or repairing a building adjoining the highway, it is his duty to provide sufficient safeguards to warn and protect passing travellers against any danger arising therefrom; and if he neglects to do so, and a traveller is injured by a falling brick, stick of timber, or otherwise, he is responsible.83

If the adjoining owner of a building suffers snow and ice to accumulate on the roof, and allows it to remain there for an unusual and unreasonable time, he is liable, if it slides off and injures a passing traveller.84 And, generally, the adjoining owner is bound to use ordinary care in maintaining his own premises in such a condition that persons lawfully using the highway may do so with safety.

The general doctrine as to the use of property is here, as elsewhere, *Sic utere tuo ut alienum non lædas,*—"So use your own property as not to injure the rights of another." If you make an excavation on your land so near to a highway that travellers are liable accidentally to fall therein, you had better surround it with a fence or other safeguard sufficient to protect reasonably the safety of travellers. If you have any passage-ways, vaults, coal-holes, flap-doors, or traps of any kind on your premises, which are dangerous for children or unwary adults, you had better abolish them, or at any rate take reasonable precaution to cover or guard them in such manner as ordinary prudence dictates, and especially if they are near the highway; for if you do not you may, some time when not convenient for you, be called upon to pay a large claim for damages or to defend yourself against an indictment. But if you have so covered and guarded them, and by the act of a trespasser, or in some other way without fault on your part, the cover, fence, or guard is removed, you are not liable until you have had actual or constructive notice of the fact, and have had reasonable opportunity to put it right.85

CHAPTER XV
PRIVATE WAYS

A private way is the right of passage over another man's land. It may be established and discontinued in the same manner as a public way, and it may also arise from necessity. A way of necessity is where a person sells land to another which is wholly surrounded by his own land, or which cannot be reached from the public highways or from the land of the purchaser. In such case the purchaser is unable to reach his land at all unless he can go over some of the surrounding estates; and inasmuch as he cannot go over the premises of those who are strangers to him, in law, and inasmuch as public policy and simple justice call for a passage-way to his land, for his use in the care and cultivation of it, the law gives him a way of necessity over his grantor's land, which runs with his land, as appurtenant thereto, so long as the necessity exists, even if nothing is said in the deed about a right of way, because it is presumed that when the grantor sells the land he intends to convey with it a right of way, without which it could not be used and enjoyed; but when the necessity ceases, the right ceases also.86 In the absence of contract, it belongs to the owner of a private way to keep it in repair,87 and for this purpose he may enter upon the way and do whatever is necessary to make it safe and convenient; but if in so doing he removes soil and stones which are not needed on the way, such surplus material belongs to the owner of the land over which the way passes.88 If a defined and designated way becomes impassable for want of repair or by natural causes, the owner of the way has not the right of a traveller on a public road to go outside the limits of the way in order to pass from one point to another.89 But if the owner of the land obstructs the way, a person entitled to use it may, without liability, enter upon and go over adjoining land of the same owner, provided he does no unnecessary damage.90 The reason for this distinction in the law between a public and a private way is that in the case of a private way the owner of the way, who alone has the right to its use, is bound to keep it in repair, whereas in the case of a public way the traveller is under no obligation to keep it in passable condition. A private way once established cannot be re-located except with the consent of both the owner of the land and of the way; but if both are agreed, the old way may be discontinued and re-located in another place.91 The owner of the soil of a private way may, the same as the owner of the fee in a highway, make any and all uses thereof to which the land can be applied.92 In the absence of agreement to the contrary, he may lawfully and without liability cover such way with a building or other structure, if he leaves a space so wide, high, and light that the way is substantially as convenient as before for the purpose for which it was established.93 And so, in the absence of agreement, he may maintain such fences across the way as are necessary to enable him to use his land for agricultural purposes, but he must provide suitable bars or gates for the use and convenience of the owner of the way. He is not required to leave it as an open way, nor to provide swing gates, if a reasonably convenient mode of passage is furnished; and if the owner of the way or his agents leave the bars or gates open, and in consequence thereof damage is done by animals, he is liable to respond in damages.94 "The law of the road" applies as well to private as to public ways, as the object of the law is to prescribe a rule of conduct for the convenience and safety of those who may have occasion to travel, and actually do travel, with carriages on a place adapted to and fitted and actually used for that purpose.95 The description of a way as a "bridle-road" does not confine the right of way to a particular class of animals or special mode of use, but it may be used for any of the ordinary purposes of a private road.96

CHAPTER XVI
DON'T

In school, church, and society many things are taught by the prohibitory don't; and thus many rules of law relating to public and private ways may be taught and illustrated in the same way. For instance:—

Don't ever drink intoxicating liquor as a beverage, at least in large quantities. If you ever have occasion to use it at all, use it very sparingly, especially if you are travelling or are about to travel with a team; for if you should collide with another team, or meet with an accident on account of a defect in the way, in a state of intoxication, your boozy condition would be some evidence that you were negligent. The law, however, is merciful and just, and if you could satisfy the court or jury that notwithstanding your unmanly condition you were using due care, and that the calamity happened through no fault of yours, you would still be entitled to a decision in your favor; but when you consider how apt a sober human mind is to think that an intoxicated mind is incapable of clear thought and intelligent action, I think you will agree with the decisions of the courts, which mean, when expressed in plain language, "You had better not be drunk when you get into trouble on the highway."97

Don't ever approach a railway crossing without looking out for the engine while the bell rings, and listening to see if the train is coming; for there is good sense as well as good law in the suggestion of Chief Baron Pollock, that a railway track *per se* is a warning of danger to those about to go upon it, and cautions them to see if a train is coming. And our court has decided that when one approaches a railway crossing he is bound to keep his eyes open, and to look up and down the rails before going upon them, without waiting for the engineer to ring the bell or to blow the whistle.98 It is a duty dictated by common sense and prudence, for one approaching a railway crossing to do so carefully and cautiously both for his own sake and the sake of those travelling by rail. If one blindly and wilfully goes upon a railway track when danger is imminent and obvious, and sustains damage, he must bear the consequences of his own rashness and folly.

Don't drive horses or other animals affected by contagious diseases on the public way, or allow them to drink at public watering-places, or keep them at home, for that matter. The common law allows a man to keep on his own premises horses afflicted with glanders, or sheep afflicted with foot-rot, or other domestic animals afflicted with any kind of diseases, provided he guards them with diligence and does not permit them to escape on to his neighbor's land or the public way. But under the statute law of this State, a man having knowledge of the existence of a contagious disease among any species of domestic animals is liable to a fine of five hundred dollars, or imprisonment for one year, if he does not forthwith inform the public authorities of such disease.99 Aside from the penalty of the statute law, it is clearly an indictable offence for any one to take domestic animals affected with contagious diseases, knowing or having reason to know them to be so affected, upon the public ways, where they are likely to give such diseases to sound animals; and he would be answerable in damages, besides.100

If you are afflicted with a contagious or infectious disease, don't expose yourself on a highway or in a public place; and don't expose another person afflicted with such disease, as thereby you may jeopardize the health of other people, and your property also, in case you should be sued by some one suffering on account of your negligence.101

When there is snow on the ground, and the movement of your sleigh is comparatively noiseless, don't drive on a public way without having at least three bells attached to some part of your harness, as that is the statute as well as the common law. By the statute law you would be liable to pay a fine of fifty dollars for each offence. And by the statute and common law, in case of a collision with another team, you would probably be held guilty of culpable negligence and made to pay heavy damages. Of course you would be allowed to show that the absence of bells on your team did not cause the accident or justify the negligence of the driver of the other team, but it would be a circumstance which would tell against you at every stage of the case.102

If you have no acquaintance with the nature and habits of horses, and no experience in driving or riding them, don't try to ride or drive any of them on a public way at first, but confine your exercise in horsemanship to your own land until you have acquired ordinary skill in their management; for the law requires every driver or rider on a highway to be reasonably proficient in the care and management of any animal he assumes to conduct through a public thoroughfare.103

Don't ride with a careless driver, if you can help it, because every traveller in a conveyance is so far identified with the one who drives or directs it, that if any injury is sustained by him by collision with another vehicle or railway train through the negligence or contributory negligence of the driver, he cannot recover damages for his injuries. The passenger, in law, is considered as being in the same position as the driver of the conveyance, and is a partaker with him in his negligence, if not in his sins.104

If you have a vicious and runaway horse, and you know it, you had better sell him, or keep him at work on the farm. Don't, at any rate, use him on the road yourself, or let him to other people to use thereon; for if in your hands he should commit injuries to person or property, you would have to foot the bills; and if he should injure the person to whom you had let him, unless you had previously informed him of the character and habits of the horse, you would be liable to pay all the damages caused by the viciousness of the horse. If you should meet with an accident by reason of a defect in the highway, you could not recover anything, however severely you might be injured or damaged, provided the vicious habits of the horse contributed to the accident.105

In riding or driving keep hold of the reins, and don't let your horses get beyond your control; for if you do your chances of victory in a lawsuit will be pretty slim. If you tie up your reins for the purpose of walking in order to get warm or to lighten the load, and let your horses go uncontrolled, and they run over a child in the road and kill it or seriously injure it, you will probably have to pay more than the value of the horses, unless they are very good ones. Or if, going thus uncontrolled, they fail to use due care and good judgment in meeting other teams, and in consequence thereof damages occur, you would be expected to make everything satisfactory, because your team is required to observe "the law of the road" whether you are with it or not, especially if you turn it loose in the highway. Even if you have hold of the reins, and your horses get beyond your control by reason of fright or other cause, and afterwards you meet with an accident by reason of a defect in the highway, you cannot recover anything.106

Don't encroach upon or abuse the highway, either by crowding fences or buildings upon its limits or by using it as a storage yard. If you set a building on the line of the road, and then put the doorsteps, the eaves, and the bow-windows of the building over the line, you are liable to an indictment for maintaining a public nuisance; and possibly you may be ordered by the court to remove them forthwith at your own expense.107 If you build an expensive bank-wall for a road fence, and place any part of it over the line, you must remove it upon the request of the public authorities, or else take your chances on an indictment for maintaining an illegal obstruction in the highway. If you deposit on the roadside logs, lumber, shingles, stones, or anything else which constitutes an obstruction to travel or a defect in the way, or which is calculated to frighten horses of ordinary gentleness, and allow the same to remain for an unreasonable length of time, you are liable to respond in damages for all injuries resulting therefrom. Even if the town should have to settle for the damages in the first instance, you might still be called upon to reimburse the town.108

Don't ride on the outside platform of a passenger coach; for if you cling upon a crowded stage-coach or street car, and voluntarily take a position in which your hold is necessarily precarious and uncertain, you have no right to complain of any accident that is the direct result of the danger to which you have seen fit to expose yourself. However, if the coach is stopped for you to get on and fare is taken for your ride, the fact that you are on the platform is not conclusive evidence against you; but the court will allow the jury to determine, upon all the evidence and under all the circumstances, whether you were in the exercise of due care, instructing them that the burden of proof is upon you to show that the injury resulted solely by the negligence of the proprietors of the coach.109

Don't jump off a passenger coach when it is in motion; for if you get off without doing or saying anything, or if you ring the bell and then get off before the coach is stopped, without any notice to those in charge of it, and without their knowing, or being negligent in not knowing, what you are doing, the coach proprietors are not liable for any injury you may receive through a fall occasioned by the sudden starting of the coach during your attempt to get off.110

Don't wilfully break down, injure, remove, or destroy a milestone, mile-board, or guide-post erected upon a public way, or wilfully deface or alter the inscription on any such stone or board, or extinguish a lamp, or break, destroy, or remove a lamp, lamp-post, railing, or posts erected on a street or other public place; for if you do you are liable to six months' imprisonment or a fine of fifty dollars.111

If in travelling you find the road impassable, or closed for repairs, and you find it convenient to turn aside and enter upon adjoining land in order to go on your way, don't be careless or imprudent; for if you take down more fences and do more damage than necessary, you may have to answer in damages to the owner of the land; and if you meet with an accident while thus out of the road, you cannot look to the town for any remuneration therefor, because when you go out of the limits of the way voluntarily, you go at your peril and on your own responsibility.112

Don't make the mistake of supposing that everything that frightens your horse or causes an accident in the highway is a defect for which the town is liable. If a town negligently suffers snowdrifts to remain in the road for a long time, and thereby you are prevented from passing over the road to attend to your business, or, in making an attempt to pass, your horses get into the snow and you are put to great trouble, expense, and loss of time in extricating them, you are remediless unless you receive some physical injury in your person or property; as the remedy provided by the statutes, in case of defects in the highway, does not extend to expenses or loss of time unless they are incident to such physical injury. In other words, the statute gives no one a claim for damages sustained in consequence of inability to use a road.113 And so a town or city is not obliged to light the highways, and an omission to do so is not a defect in the way for which it is liable.114

Nor is the mere narrowness and crookedness of a road a defect within the meaning of the statutes. Towns and cities are only required to keep highways in suitable repair as they are located by the public authorities, and they have no right to go outside the limits defined by the location in order to make the road more safe and convenient for travel. If a highway is so narrow or crooked as to be unsafe, the proper remedy is by an application to the county commissioners to widen or straighten it.115 Nor is smooth and slippery ice, in country road or city street, a defect for which a town or city is liable, if the road whereon the ice accumulates is reasonably level and well constructed. In our climate the formation of thin but slippery ice over the whole surface of the ground is frequently only the work of a few hours; and to require towns and cities to remove this immediately or at all is supposing that the legislature intended to cast upon them a duty impossible to perform, and a burden beyond their ability to carry.116

If you meet with an accident on the highway by reason of a defect therein, don't fail to give notice in writing within thirty days, to the county, town, place, or persons by law obliged to keep said highway in repair, stating the time, place, and cause of the injury or damage.117 This notice is a condition precedent to the right to maintain an action for such injury or damage, and cannot be waived by the city or town.118 Nothing will excuse such notice except the physical or mental incapacity of the person injured, in which case he may give the notice within ten days after such incapacity is removed, and in case of his death it may be given by his executors or administrators.119 Formerly it was essential that the time, place, and cause of the injury should be set forth in the notice with considerable particularity, but now the notice is not invalid by reason of any inaccuracy in stating the time, place, and cause, if the error is not intentional and the party entitled to notice is not misled.120

Don't convey by warranty deed a piece of land over which there is a public or a private way, without conveying subject to such way; for if you do you may be called upon to make up the difference in value in the land with the incumbrance upon it and with it off, which is regarded as a just compensation for the injury resulting from such an incumbrance.121

Finally, don't keep a dog that is in the habit of running into the road and barking at passing teams. You had better get rid of him or break him of the habit. Under our statutes the owner or keeper of a dog is responsible to any person injured by him, either in person or property, double the amount of damage sustained; and after he has received notice of the bad disposition of his dog, he is liable to have the damage increased threefold.

Every dog that has the habit of barking at people on the highway is liable any day to subject his owner or keeper to large liabilities; for if he frightens a horse by leaping or barking at him in mere play, and the horse runs away, or tips over the vehicle to which he is hitched, his owner or keeper is responsible for double the damages thus caused by his dog. Hence I repeat the injunction, Get rid of such a dog or break him of the habit; and if this cannot be done, then break his neck.

Perhaps it might be well to say, in this connection, that any traveller on the road, either riding or walking peaceably, who is suddenly assaulted by a dog, whether licensed or not, may legally kill him, and thus relieve his owner or keeper of a disagreeable duty.122

CHAPTER XVII
FOOT-PATHS

Air, sunlight, and exercise are absolutely essential for the proper physical and intellectual development of human beings. Thoreau thought it necessary for people who wished to preserve their health and spirits to spend four hours a day in the open air, sauntering through the woods and over the hills and fields, free from all worldly engagements. No doubt he spoke from his own personal standpoint, and many persons do not require so much exercise in the open air as he did in order to preserve their health and spirits; but the proper observance of the laws of health certainly requires every one to spend a portion of every pleasant day in the open air, and on foot if possible. Since the morning stars first sang together, the whole creation has been groaning and travailing in preparing the earth for the habitation of man; and the influence and teachings of Nature have ever aided powerfully in perfecting man and upbuilding the ruling nations of the world.

The progenitors of every vigorous race have always found in forest and wilderness the tonics and sources of their strength. It took forty years of wandering in the wilderness to prepare the Israelites for the occupation of the promised land. In the open and out-door life of the Athenians was developed a civilization noble in high aspirations for the ideal in beauty and life, rich in literary and oratorical achievements, and glorious in the great and profound thoughts of immortal teachers and philosophers. The august and all-conquering civilization of the Romans had its origin on Palatine Hill when herdsmen and wolves roamed over it. In Holland, where the people are ever in conflict with the elements of Nature, the land has been reclaimed by human effort from "the multitudinous waves of the sea." The streams that once spread over the land or hid themselves in quicksands and thickets are made to flow in channels and form a network of watery highways for commerce and the fertilization of the soil; and where formerly lagoons and morasses found a home, there are now pleasant homesteads, great cities, and beautiful villages. The Anglo-Saxon race, which is now and has been for centuries the most vigorous and progressive in the world, has always had an insatiable hunger for the earth, and a love for a life in the fields by stream or by roadside. Everywhere we find the highest type of civilization where man has gained the mastery of Nature by the work of his hands. The home of such a civilization is usually found where forests have been removed, and the wild vegetation of primitive times has been expelled to make room for the thousand and one productions of modern cultivation; where hillsides and mountain-cliffs have been festooned with vines and made to blossom like the rose; where watercourses have been made highways for trade and utilized for purposes of manufacture; and where gloomy morasses and damp lowlands have been dried up and made fertile and habitable by drainage and cultivation.

As close contact with Nature is necessary for the making of nations, so her teachings are essential for the largest expansion of the human mind. All the great teachers of the race have found in Nature the germs of the thoughts which have widened the bounds of human knowledge "with the process of the suns." "Speak to the earth, and it will teach thee," was the basis of Job's philosophy. When David wanted light and assistance, he lifted up his eyes unto the hills, from whence came his help. Plato taught in the consecrated groves of the Academy, and Aristotle in the pleasant fields of Nymphäeum or in the shady walks of the Lyceum. Christ taught his disciples to heed the teachings of Nature, and he sought strength and inspiration in the wilderness and the mountains. Wordsworth's library was in his house, but his study was out of doors. But why enumerate, when the entire intellectual history of our race demonstrates that every invention or thought which has extended man's mental vision and knowledge has been evolved from the discovery of some hitherto hidden law of the material world, or from the teachings of Nature, which always foreshadow the fundamental principles regnant in the seen and the unseen world? Hence anything which tends to bring people into the open air and into a closer communion with Nature is worthy of encouragement.

Good foot-paths would furnish an easy and convenient way of getting at Nature; and being free from the dust and heat of the highway, and somewhat retired and secluded, they would be, during a considerable portion of the year, musical with the song of birds and beautiful with green foliage and lovely flowers. These paths would invite and encourage people to take long walks, and this habit would undoubtedly conduce to their longevity and robust health. And the promotion of health is now regarded, in every enlightened community, as one of the objects of government. The enjoyment of life depends in great measure upon the state of our health. When the air feels bracing, and food and drink taste sweet to us, much else in life tastes sweet which would otherwise taste sour and disagreeable. Good drainage and vaccination are not the only means available for the promotion of the public health. People should be encouraged and educated into the habit of taking plenty of exercise in the open air, as in this way the public health will be improved.

One of the charms of old England is to be found in her numerous foot-paths and green lanes, which are recognized by law, for many of them are older than the highways. When a walker tires of the public road or is in a hurry, if he knows the country, he can turn into some foot-path and reach the place of his destination by short cuts through green lanes, across pleasant meadows, and along shady hedgerows. As one passes along these cosey byways, he sees, from every eminence or turn, a new prospect over the landscape interspersed with trees, now and then the bright gleam of water through the foliage, and occasionally some beautiful vista view across parks and homesteads. In this way one can go from town to town, and get about the country quite independently of the highways. Most of the country churches are approachable by lanes and foot-paths which seem to run by all the houses in the vicinage, and by their sweet attractiveness to invite all the people to go to church, at least in pleasant summer weather.

In Massachusetts and some of the other States, towns and cities have authority to lay out foot-paths in the same manner as public ways. It is to be hoped ere-long that the intelligent and public-spirited citizens of our towns and cities will cause now and then a good foot-walk to be constructed, where it would shorten the distance from one place to another, and possibly pass through pleasant fields and woods, and over hills commanding beautiful and extensive views. It is not pleasant to walk in the dust and publicity of highways, nor on gravel walks in artificial parks, where sign-boards and policemen warn you frequently to "keep off the grass."

Before our towns and cities spend any more money building boulevards and opening new parks, would it not be well for them to consider the advisability of laying out some foot-paths for the comfort and convenience of pedestrians? At any rate, foot-paths could be made alongside of the road-bed of some of the public ways, so that every pedestrian would not of necessity have to trudge along in the dust or mud incident to the middle of the road.

CHAPTER XVIII
WITHIN AND WITHOUT THE ROADSIDE

Besides the legal duty every dweller by a highway is under, to use it with due regard to the rights of the public, he is under a moral and Christian obligation to maintain order and neatness within and without his roadside. The occupations and amenities of life are so interwoven and intermixed that no one can live for himself alone with justice to himself or to society. There is something in the very nature of things which makes for the reward of unselfish exertion and for the condemnation of selfish acts. "Whosoever shall seek to save his life, shall lose it; and whosoever shall lose his life, shall preserve it." Public spirit, like virtue, is its own exceeding great reward. When one benefits the community in which he lives, he thereby also benefits himself; and when he is possessed of the right kind of a public spirit, he will beautify and improve his homestead and his roadside, and will even throw the cobble-stones out of the roadway in front of his house without compensation or even hope of financial reward.

When he plants a tree for the sole purpose of doing something for posterity, and then watches its growth and expansion from day to day until he becomes familiar with its varied aspects in sunny and in stormy weather, and finally, walking beneath its cooling shade and seeing its limbs swaying gracefully over surrounding objects, his heart goes out towards it with a feeling of tenderness and love, and he feels that he has been paid a thousand times for setting it out. When after years of endeavor in trying to keep his roadside neat and clean and covered with greensward, he finds that his example is having some influence on his neighbors, and that even the road-menders begin to respect his efforts to improve the wayside, he feels that he has been amply compensated for all his trouble and care in his own increased enjoyment and in the increased enjoyment he has been the means of giving to the public.

First impressions always have great influence upon our minds. Nothing will give a traveller a poorer and meaner opinion of a town and its inhabitants than dilapidated buildings surrounded by rubbish and broken-down fences.

When a traveller passes a house of this character, he instinctively says to himself, "Some shiftless and poverty-stricken family lives here;" but when he passes a well-kept house with pleasant surroundings, he says, "This must be the abode of intelligent and well-to-do people." He feels like stopping and forming their acquaintance, for he is sure that their acquaintance would be worth having. Our opinion of a person's character is always more or less influenced by the clothes he wears and by the house in which he lives. The surroundings of every home of intelligence and tidiness should indicate that it is not the abode of the vulgar and ignorant. Therefore every owner of a homestead should strive to make it a cosey and pleasant home for himself and family. He should take a just pride in keeping his buildings in good repair, well painted and suitably arranged for the purposes of his business and a happy and healthy home life. The surroundings should be made neat and attractive, by the absence of rubbish, and the presence of green grass and shade trees.

If he owns much land, he ought to be landscape gardener enough to set out his fruit and shade trees and to lay out his fields in the best way for convenience and scenic effect. He should also have sufficient rural taste not to locate his barn and other out-buildings in such a way as to shut off the best views from his house. He ought also to have a general knowledge of the nature and uses of trees and forests, and the necessity of their cultivation for the good of himself and mankind at large.

Forest and shade trees greatly enhance the beauties of a country, and no country can be beautiful in the highest degree without them. If the green hills and mountains of New England were stripped of their woods, the lovers of natural scenery and rural life would seek elsewhere the gratification of their tastes. Even the stately homes of England would appear commonplace in the absence of the majestic trees and forests which now encircle them. A plain, modest house, situated in the midst of an open grass-plat and sheltered by a few handsome shade trees, is more beautiful and appeals more strongly to the feelings than the stateliest mansion unprotected from the sun. Who would care to live by the side of the purest stream or body of water, if it were not fringed with trees? Were it not for trees, would there be any beauty in mountain, hill, or valley,—for who can conceive of a beautiful landscape scene devoid of trees?

The love of trees seems to be implanted in all noble natures. The ancients believed that "the groves were the first temples of the gods." Christopher North says that the man who loves not trees would make no bones of murdering.

Some people give as an excuse for not planting trees that it takes so long for them to grow that they will not live to enjoy them. The selfishness of this excuse is enough to condemn it; but it is not tenable from any point of view. It has been said that he who makes two blades of grass grow where only one grew before is a benefactor of his race; and of all the pursuits connected with the interests of mankind what can be the source of more true and disinterested happiness than the knowledge that one has been instrumental in changing a waste and unproductive piece of land into a scene of umbrageous and waving beauty? Cicero speaks of tree-planting as the most delightful occupation of advanced life; and Sir Robert Walpole once said that among the various actions of his busy life none had given him so much satisfaction in the performance and so much unsullied pleasure in the retrospect as the planting with his own hands many of those magnificent trees that now form the pride of Houghton.

Of course it is not claimed that every one should have expensive buildings upon his homestead, or wide-spreading lawns around his house. Many are so situated that they cannot afford to live in costly houses or to spend much money on their surroundings; but every one can make his home, however humble, pleasant and homelike, and can keep his dooryard and wayside free from old rubbish. I can understand how love can be happy in a cottage, but I do not believe it possible for a family to grow in knowledge and virtue and enjoy life while dwelling in mean and dirty apartments.

Cleanliness is next to godliness, and it is just as true of the outside of the house as of the inside. A pleasant and beautiful exterior usually signifies pleasantness and peace within. While well-fenced and well-tilled farms are always pleasing to the eyesight, and neatly dressed roadsides are generally desirable, it does not follow that no shrubbery or sylvan tangles of trees should be allowed to grow on farms or by the wayside. A bare and rocky hill or knoll suggests images of bleak and barren desolation, cold blasts, and parching sun; while a hill clothed and capped with woods gives the impression of a rich and charming country. Therefore the land unsuitable for pasturage or cultivation on a farm had better be covered with clusters of trees or with forests; and frequently an old stone-wall or heaps of stones can be advantageously hidden by vines and shrubbery, as they add beauty to the landscape, furnish shelter to birds, and often protect the crops from cold winds. Many a wayside in country by-roads is so rough and uneven, so rocky and full of earth-pits, that it had better be covered with the wild shrubbery of Nature than to be cleared up in such a way as to expose to view all its unsightly objects. Whenever the roadside cannot be covered by greensward, the native shrubs and wild vines ought to be allowed to hide its nakedness with green foliage and beautiful flowers. They give beauty to wayside scenery, and increase the interest and pleasure of those travelling along the road.

CHAPTER XIX
ENJOYMENT OF THE ROAD

In travelling, whether one is riding or walking, it is not sufficient for the proper enjoyment of the way to know how to get along in a legal manner, but he should know how to put himself in harmony with the elements of Nature, and to feel the "gay, fresh sentiment of the road." The first requisite for this enjoyment is to have a hopeful and sunshiny disposition. When people are buoyed up by hope they will find enjoyment under very adverse circumstances. Adam and Eve, according to Milton, saw without terror for the first time the sun descend beneath the horizon, and the darkness close in upon the earth, and "the firmament glow with living sapphires," although they did not then know of a sunrise to come. Yet even in such a time as that, according to this poet, these hopeful natures walked hand in hand "in the grateful evening mild," and held such sweet converse with each other that they forgot all time, all seasons and their change, for all pleased alike. Thus it was in the beginning, and thus it will be at the end; for even in the darkest as in the brightest hours hopeful humanity looks forward to something better, as—

> "Of better and brighter days to come
> Man is talking and dreaming ever."

And who would have it otherwise? As sunshine is the most important thing in the natural world, so it is the best thing in human life. People with sunshiny dispositions are always happy and welcome everywhere, whether on the road, in the sick-room, or in the halls of gayety. They drive away the blues and bring in hope and good cheer; without them, life would not be worth living.

The French philosopher Figuier was so impressed with the value of sunshine in human nature that he taught that the rays of the sun, which bring light and heat and life and all blessings to the earth, are nothing but the loving emanations of the just spirits who have reached the sun, the final abode of all immortal souls; and its light and heat are the result of their effulgent goodness and sunshiny dispositions.

Every traveller, then, who wishes to experience even the common and apparent enjoyments of the way, should start out with a light heart and rich in hope; but if he wishes to taste also the *latent* enjoyments of the way, he must have an observing eye, and the love of Nature in his heart. It is astonishing how the systematic cultivation of the observing faculties will develop in one the habit of seeing and enjoying his environment. This habit grows as rapidly as heavenly wisdom in one who has made an honest attempt to obtain a knowledge of God, when—

"Each faculty tasked to perceive Him
Has gained an abyss where a dewdrop was asked."

What a source of pleasure, solace, and recreation, then, is open to him who knows how to distinguish and appreciate the beautiful in Nature! He hears in every breeze and every ripple of water a voice which the uncultivated ear cannot hear; and he sees in every fleeting cloud and varied aspect of Nature some beauty which the ignorant cannot see.

"Earth's crammed with heaven,
And every common bush afire with God;
But only he who sees takes off his shoes."

There is truth in the quaint language of Platen: "The more things thou learnest to know and to enjoy, the more complete and full will be for thee the delight of living."

We frequently find that when two persons are placed in the same situation, one will find much to enjoy while the other will not, and simply because one has the love of Nature in his heart, and the other has not. One person, living in the midst of the most beautiful natural scenery, is not charmed by anything he sees on the earth or in the sky. To him all Nature is like an empty barnyard, in which there is nothing to inspire him with a noble thought or stir him with a generous emotion. Another person living in the same vicinity sees much in his surroundings to admire and to enjoy. He looks at the sunset glows with delight; he sees beauty in the grass, and glory in the flowers; he sees with admiration and awe the storm-clouds, black and terrible, rushing together like veritable war-horses, or piling themselves up like mountains, reverberating with the artillery of heaven and tongued with fire; wherever he looks nearly every prospect pleases; and to him Nature, like the Scriptures, is new every morning and new every night. Such a person is more likely to be a better neighbor, a better citizen, and a better Christian than one who has not the love of Nature in his heart. Ruskin says: "The love of Nature is an invariable sign of goodness of heart and justice of moral perception; that in proportion to the degree in which it is felt, will probably be the degree in which all nobleness and beauty of character will also be felt; that when it is absent from any mind, that mind in many other respects is hard, worldly, and degraded." The love of Nature has ever been characteristic of the greatest and the noblest minds. To Wordsworth the meanest flower that blows gave him thoughts too deep for tears; and to Christ the lily of the field was more beautifully arrayed than Solomon in all his glory. Likewise we often find that two travellers will pass together over the same route, and one will see much to admire and to enjoy by the way, and the other will see nothing to admire or to enjoy. The one who has an observing eye, and enjoys beautiful and grand natural scenery, sees in every nook and corner by the way some lovely flower or comely shrub to admire, and, like Wordsworth,—

"Beside the lake, beneath the trees,
Fluttering and dancing in the breeze,
He sees the golden daffodils."

And he not only enjoys the present sight, but he enjoys the scene as often as he thinks of it afterwards, as in imagination he views the scene over and over again,—

"For oft when on his couch he lies
In vacant or in pensive mood,
They flash upon the inward eye
Which is the bliss of solitude;
And then his heart with pleasure fills,
And dances with the daffodils."

And in the common and unnoticed grass by the roadside or in the field, he can see in each blade a system of masonry and architecture that no human skill has ever been able to equal. The stem is very slender, but is so elastic and strong that it waves gracefully in the breeze and bends to the earth in the storm without breaking, and assumes an upright attitude again. It is made up of delicate cells and perfect and intricate channels, through which hidden currents of life throb and flow as mysteriously as the vital blood through the human frame. It is colored with an emerald tint of such beautiful hues that it has been the despair of artists to imitate it in every age. Ages and ages before the human hand learned its cunning, the command went forth for grass to bring forth seed after its kind; and to-day it is waving gracefully in every field, and crowned with the same beautiful flowers and tasselled seed-vessels as of old. Men in their haughty ambition have builded much larger structures. They have erected towers, pyramids, obelisks, spires, monuments, and triumphal arches, which have commanded the admiration of their builders and of their fellow-men in every part of the world; but every principle of their masonry and architecture is an imitation of that in the humblest spear of grass. Thus every traveller on a country road is surrounded by monuments more ancient, more impressive, and more beautiful than the ancient or modern world can show as the production of human hands.

He finds much enjoyment in the study of the forms and characteristics of the different trees by the wayside. If the road passes over highland, on a breezy day he can look down upon or across the tops of undulating forest trees, whose swaying movements remind him of the waves of the sea. He can see in each species not only a variety in the color and form of its foliage, but some characteristic which reminds him of some human being. The rugged oak or apple tree recalls to his mind some sturdy man, of great strength and honesty of character, with picturesque but awkward manners. The gracefully swaying branches of the stately elm or weeping willow remind him of some woman whose elegant form and manners make her as lovely as the moon and as beautiful as light. The rapid and constant motion of the foliage of the poplar and the aspen reminds him of some nervous and excitable person who is never quiet or easy for a moment. The prim spruce-tree suggests to him some person of formal habits and primness of dress. The symmetrical maple and pine remind him of some quiet and dignified character who is well balanced and rounded at every point. The patriarchal tree which has outlived all its companions and stands alone with few and withered branches, but still raising its majestic head to heaven as if in supplication for blessings on the earth, reminds him of some gray-haired person who, full of years and rich in faith, after a well-spent life is approaching and can almost see the other side of the river which separates this life from the eternal world.

If he has a taste for domestic and pastoral scenery, it is gratified as he views the green pastures and meadows, the waving grain-fields, and the occasional gleam of water through the foliage. Ever and anon he passes by some dwelling where the charms of culture have been added to the charms of Nature. By kind treatment the grass-plat before the door has become a refreshing piece of verdure. By careful pruning and training the trees on the lawn have become objects of beauty, and cast their graceful shadows over the velvety greensward beneath. The woodbine tastefully trained over the porch, the flower-bed in the yard brilliant with flowers, and the garden and the fruit orchard in the field, all tend to cheer and sanctify human life in such an abode. Perchance the road runs by some rural homestead which reminds him of his own ancestral home, humble yet beautiful to him, and all the scenes of his childhood come vividly to mind as fond recollection presents them to view. He is once more a barefoot boy, and all is outward sunshine and inward joy. He slacks his thirst once more from the well by the door or at the spring on the hillside; and he visits again the old familiar play-ground, the lane through which the cows are driven, the brook where the sheep are washed, the fish are caught, and the boys go in swimming.

When the road leads him into the mountains or in sight of them, he is charmed by their majesty and awed by their sublimity. A mountain panorama presents all the characteristic phases of Nature and all the moving variation of the atmosphere. At one time they are cloud-capped and surrounded with fog, and then in an incredibly short time they are glittering in a halo of sunlight. As one beholds their majestic heads, around which the storms of centuries have beat, disappear as twilight changes into night, he can but feel oppressed with the gloom and melancholy of the scene. But in the morning, when—

> "Night's candles are burnt out, and jocund day
> Stands tiptoe on the misty mountain-tops,"

he can but conclude with Ruskin, that "mountain scenery has been prepared in order to unite as far as possible and in the closest compass every means of delighting and sanctifying the heart of man. Mountains seem to have been built for the human race, as at once their schools and cathedrals, full of treasures of illuminated manuscript for the scholar, kindly in simple lessons to the worker, quiet in pale cloisters for the thinker, glowing in holiness for the worshipper."

Then, again, a country road is a good place to become acquainted with some forms of animal and vegetable life. The odors of growing vegetation, the movement of squirrels and other creatures, and the song of birds, all have a tendency to impress one with the idea that the material world is animated with life. And when the sun pours down a flood of glowing sunlight, and swathes the traveller and the whole world with its glowing and life-giving beams, he realizes that the sun is the source of every material blessing. In the city people know in a general way that the sun is the source of heat and light, and that he adds to their comfort and convenience, as do the electric light and the fire on the hearth; but they hardly realize that his rays are necessary for their existence, to say nothing of their comfort, for even a week. But when a traveller in the morning sees all animated Nature stirring and rejoicing with the throbbings of warmed and rejuvenated life; when he looks out over the landscape and sees the sun raising in misty vapors the water which supplies our springs, lakes, and streams, and refreshes the earth in showers of rain, he realizes that the sun is not only the fire which warms the world, but it is also the mighty hydraulic engine of Nature.

These are some of the enjoyments of the way; but every thoughtful and observing traveller knows that they cannot be enumerated. Like Burroughs, "he is not isolated, but one with things, with the farms and industries on either hand. The vital, universal currents play through him. He knows the ground is alive: he feels the pulses of the wind, and reads the mute language of things. His sympathies are all aroused; his senses are continually reporting messages to his mind. Wind, frost, rain, heat, cold, are something to him. He is not merely a spectator of the panorama of Nature, but a participator in it. He experiences the country he passes through,—tastes it, feels it, absorbs it."

Neither is he confined to the material demonstrations of Nature for his enjoyment of the way. Some of the greatest sermons and speeches have been thought out on the road. A solitary traveller can think calmly and thoughtfully on the great problems of life and death, and can learn to appreciate the fact that "the gods approve the depth, and not the tumult, of the soul."

FOOTNOTES

1 11 Allen, 530.

2 Pub. St. c. 49, § 94.

3 128 Mass. 63.

4 7 Cush. 394.

5 5 Pick. 492.

6 14 Gray, 214.

7 4 Cush. 291.

8 6 Met. 329.

9 Pub. St. c. 49, § 99.

10 13 Gray, 601.

11 Pub. St. c. 52, § 12.

12 St. 1885, c. 123.

13 . St. c. 54.

14 Pub. St. c. 54.

15 125 Mass. 216.

16 128 Mass. 546.

17 8 Allen, 473.

18 13 Allen, 429.

19 122 Mass. 389.

20 3 Allen, 374; 8 Allen, 237.

21 100 Mass. 49.

22 98 Mass. 578.

23 Pub. St. c. 53, §§ 1-5.

24 Pub. St. c. 217; 108 Mass. 140.

25 Pub. St. c. 27, § 50.

26 125 Mass. 526.

27 St. 1885, c. 123.

28 Pub. St. c. 54, § 6.

29 St. 1885, c. 157.

30 Pub. St. c. 54, §§ 7, 8.

31 Pub. St. c. 54, §§ 10, 11.

32 4 Gray, 178.

33 8 Allen, 522.

34 3 Cush. 300; 114 Mass. 518.

35 1 Addison on Torts, 466.

36 Pub. St. c. 93.

37 Angell on Highways, § 336.

38 Shear. & Red. on Negligence, § 309.

39 121 Mass. 216.

40 12 Met. 415.

41 10 Cush. 495; 3 Carr. & Payne, 554; Angell on Carriers, § 555.

42 12 Allen, 84.

43 4 Pick. 125; 8 Met. 213.

44 111 Mass. 360.

45 Pub. St. c. 113, § 37; 7 Allen, 573.

46 24 Wend. 465.

47 23 Penn. St. 196.

48 5 Carr. & Payne, 407.

49 1 Allen, 180.

50 1 Addison on Torts, § 480.

51 14 Allen, 475; Barker v. Worcester, 139 Mass. 74.

52 9 Met. 1.

53 103 Mass. 391.

54 1 Watts, Pa. 360.

55 Pub. St. c. 202, § 34.

56 Pub. St. c. 202, § 35.

57 35 N. H. 257.

58 136 Mass. 75.

59 14 Gray, 242.

60 106 Mass. 281; 126 Mass. 506.

61 30 Q. B. Ont. 41.

62 2 F. & F. 229.

63 3 Salk. 183.

64 Pub. St. c. 27, § 15, and c. 53; 97 Mass. 221.

65 136 Mass. 75.

66 St. 1884, c. 306.

67 15 Johns, 447.

68 107 Mass. 414.

69 4 Gray, 215; 136 Mass. 10.

70 6 Mass. 454.

71 16 Mass. 33; 8 Allen, 473.

72 Pub. St. c. 53, § 10.

73 38 Me. 195.

74 24 Pick. 187.

75 1 Cush. 443; 13 Met. 115; 107 Mass. 264; 14 Gray, 75; Pub. St. c. 112, § 17.

76 4 Allen, 444.

77 10 Cox, 102.

78 25 Me. 538.

79 114 Mass. 466.

80 7 Cush. 408.

81 134 Mass. 522.

82 13 Allen, 211, 291; 136 Mass. 119.

83 123 Mass. 26.

84 101 Mass. 251; 106 Mass. 194.

85 4 Carr. & Payne, 262, 337; 51 N.Y. 229; 19 Conn. 507.

86 14 Mass. 49; 2 Met. 457; 14 Gray, 126.

87 12 Mass. 65.

88 10 Gray, 65.

89 Wash, on Ease. *196.

90 2 Allen, 543.

91 5 Gray, 409; 14 Gray, 473.

92 Wash, on Ease. *196.

93 2 Met. 457.

94 31 N. Y 366; 44 N. H. 539; 4 M. & W. 245.

95 23 Pick. 201.

96 16 Gray, 175.

97 3 Allen, 402; 115 Mass. 239.

98 12 Met. 415.

99 St. 1885, c. 148.

100 2 Rob. N.Y. 326; 16 Conn. 200.

101 4 M. & S. 73; Wood on Nuisances, 70.

102 12 Met. 415; 11 Gray, 392; 8 Allen, 436.

103 2 Lev. 173.

104 Addison on Torts, § 479.

105 4 Gray, 478; 117 Mass. 204.

106 101 Mass. 93; 106 Mass. 278; 40 Barb. 193.

107 107 Mass. 234.

108 Wood on Nuisances, §§ 326, 327; 102 Mass. 341; 18 Me. 286; 41 Vt. 435.

109 103 Mass. 391; 8 Allen, 234; 115 Mass. 239.

110 106 Mass. 463.

111 Pub. St. c. 203, § 76.

112 8 Met. 391; 7 Cush. 408; 7 Barb. 309.

113 13 Met. 297; 6 Cush. 141.

114 136 Mass. 419.

115 105 Mass. 473.

116 12 Allen, 566; 102 Mass. 329; 104 Mass. 78.

117 Pub. St. c. 52, §§ 19-21.

118 128 Mass. 387.

119 Pub. St. c. 52, § 21.

120 St. 1882, c. 36.

121 2 Mass. 97; 15 Pick. 66; 2 Allen, 428.

122 11 Gray, 29; 1 Allen, 191; 3 Allen, 191.